HOMELAND CALLING

WORDS FROM A NEW GENERATION OF ABORIGINAL AND TORRES STRAIT ISLANDER VOICES

Aboriginal and Torres Strait Islander readers are advised that this book may contain images and names of people who have died

First published in 2020 by Hardie Grant Explore, a division of Hardie Grant Publishing
Last updated in [February, 2024].

Hardie Grant Explore (Melbourne)
Wurundjeri Country
Building 1, 658 Church Street
Richmond, Victoria 3121

Hardie Grant Explore (Sydney)
Gadigal Country
Level 7, 45 Jones Street
Ultimo, NSW 2007

www.hardiegrant.com/au/explore

Hardie Grant acknowledges the Traditional Owners of the Country on which we work, the Wurundjeri People of the Kulin Nation and the Gadigal People of the Eora Nation, and recognises their continuing connection to the land, waters and culture. We pay our respects to their Elders past and present.

NATIONAL LIBRARY OF AUSTRALIA

A catalogue record for this book is available from the National Library of Australia

Homeland Calling
ISBN 9781741176926

10 9 8 7 6 5 4 3

Publisher: Melissa Kayser
Editor: Ellen van Neerven
Editorial assistant: Jessica Smith
Design: Erika Budiman
Artist: Lakkari Pitt
Prepress: Splitting Image Colour Studio, Erika Budiman

Background cover image sourced from iStock.com/manuel_adorf

Printed in Australia by Opus Group Pty Ltd, an Accredited ISO AS/NZS 14001 Environmental Management System printer.

FSC www.fsc.org MIX Paper | Supporting responsible forestry FSC® C018684

The paper this book is printed on is certified against the Forest Stewardship Council® Standards. Griffin Press – a member of the Opus Group – holds chain of custody certification SCS-COC-001185. FSC® promotes environmentally responsible, socially beneficial and economically viable management of the world's forests.

HOMELAND CALLING

EDITED BY
ELLEN VAN NEERVEN

FOREWORD BY
DANZAL BAKER AKA BAKER BOY

ARTWORK BY
LAKKARI PITT

PRESENTED BY
DESERT PEA MEDIA

Hardie Grant
EXPLORE

DESERT PEA MEDIA

CONTENTS

FOREWORD

I grew up with dance and music. My grandmother had travelled Australia and the world dancing and performing, with my grandfather always following and documenting her journey, so that they could pass that onto their children and then onto me, my siblings and cousins. It's something I hope to one day pass onto my kids, too. I have fond memories of dancing as a kid. Dancing with my dad and uncles who were the original 'Baker Boys'. Dancing on tables in free time at school, and not understanding why my teacher wasn't impressed with my stage show. I lived for dance, for entertaining.

My love for dance led me on a journey to follow in my dad's footsteps, as he had followed in my grandmother's footsteps, by travelling Australia to perform and teach. I have visited over 250 regional and remote Indigenous communities in the space of three years, where we taught healthy lifestyles through hip-hop dance and music. We worked with the young people to encourage them to write music in their First language, and that's where my story as the Baker Boy you know today began.

I was there encouraging those kids to use their First language, but hadn't taken that advice on myself. During some downtime with one of my brother boys, who's an incredible lyricist and can freestyle like no-one else I know, he was challenging me to do the same as him. But I felt shame because I didn't feel like my English was good enough, and I couldn't come up with the words quickly like he did. Instead of laughing at me, he sent me away and encouraged me to write in language, just as we were encouraging the kids in the communities we visited to do. I went away, and I wrote. Those first bars, first lyrics I ever wrote turned into what became my first single 'Cloud 9'. I would never have written or felt the confidence to share this work if it wasn't for the encouragement of the incredible people around me and their words. They were simple words, but they were words that created a new pathway for me.

At first, I didn't think what I'd written was a big deal. I didn't think anyone was ever going to listen to it. It was just a fun project that I made and was proud of. But it quickly blew up, and I was launched into this world of music and performing and rapping in both English and Yolŋu Matha.

Initially I didn't realise the power of what I was doing; to me, speaking more than one language is normal. But the more I travel and perform, the more I realise the importance of spreading the word of First languages. I've met and performed for so many people who didn't know where Arnhem Land was, who didn't realise the First people of Australia spoke languages other than English, and how many thousands of languages and dialects there are, and how many more there used to be, that we have now lost.

I realised that rapping in my First language in mainstream music empowered me to educate non-Indigenous Australians about the oldest surviving culture on earth. I could use my music to open up people's eyes to see our First people as more than the stereotypes they have been taught.

And for my fellow brothers and sisters, I could show them that we are strong, we are beautiful and we should be proud of our culture, our stories, our languages. I hope that I can inspire people, no matter where they are from or where they grew up, and however they identify, that they should be proud of who they are, and celebrate that every day.

I am so honoured to have the platform I do to be able to share and give back. No matter where my music career goes, I will always use performance and language to educate and share with the world the beauty of Indigenous Australia, our culture, our communities, our LANGUAGES.

Danzal Baker aka Baker Boy

INTRODUCTION

Looking through the pages of this beautiful book brings back such a flood of warm memories. It's been a genuine privilege, and a joy, to spend the past eighteen years learning, connecting, sharing and creating with Original Nations young people, community members and knowledge holders in hundreds of communities all around Australia.

We are ecstatic to see this poetry, these stories here in one place.

These are songs created in collaboration with young people, Elders and communities, waves of words and sounds that have rippled out from country, from homelands, reserves, missions, communities, towns and cities all across Australia. In the pages of this book, they will now be preserved on coffee tables, on bookshelves and in libraries, and the stories in the songs will be heard and understood, in a different way, by even more people.

Listening is a fundamental part of the Desert Pea Media creative process. We create spaces for young people, to find, express and elevate their unique perspective and voice. When you listen to the music, beyond the captivating visuals, you hear their own words reinforcing their motivation, self-worth and pride in identity, culture and country. To have the opportunity to amplify these important words even further, here, has been an unexpected and wonderful thing.

We respect, value and stand behind the voices of our Original Nations young people, and it is a pleasure to present to you this collection of important works. Through this book their stories are shared and now all Australians have the opportunity to know and understand. We hope you will enjoy them, and share them around.

Toby Finlayson
Creative Director
Desert Pea Media

EDITOR'S INTRODUCTION

Hey you mob,

Are you ready to go on a journey around the country and witness the finest young hip-hop lyricists out there? You wanna go to Cowra, Forbes, Mer, Palm, Mully and Wilcannia? These young brothers and sisters are the future, their passion for their homelands is electric, it's epic.

We firstly have to acknowledge the Ancestors and the Elders that inform us as younger people, and who have got us to where we are today, as well as acknowledging the country we are on.

These groups of young lyricists will make you proud, hey. Young voices, but at the same time so old because of hundreds of years of culture behind them.

Homeland Calling is broken up into four sections using titles from the songs themselves: 'country is my heartbeat', about environment and place; 'history is in my bloodline', about knowledge and survival; 'flame in the struggle', about mental health and wellbeing; and 'pride in my people', about family and community. These themes are important to every Aboriginal and Torres Strait Islander I know, as they are embedded in our values and overlap each other.

You can read these powerful words by themselves. Or you can decide to listen and watch the songs, and sing along with the words in front of you.

I'm Mununjali Yugambeh mob from the Scenic Rim in south-east Queensland, and it was my absolute pleasure to help bring these words together in solidarity with young black Australia. I will keep returning to these words and songs whenever I need strength.

The future is here. Get into this you mob.

Love,
Ellen xo

I | COUNTRY IS MY HEARTBEAT

HEARTBEAT

» WILCANNIA BARKINDJI SOLDIERS

» we belong to where the Baaka* flow
even when the Baaka* low
no matter which country I roam
my heartbeat never far from home

wiimpitcha* ... baakantji* ... murlpa* ... kiiranha*
my people of the red dust country
river red gum
mission to the Mallee back to Stress Street
get 'em up
this my mob, this is me, this my future
set 'em up

I'm connected to my country
to my culture to my mob
when the river down
my people disconnect, get on the grog

I'm connected to my country
to my culture, to my health
if you disrespect your country
then you disrespect yourself

country is my medicine
fire is light
country is my heartbeat
water is life

wiimpitcha murndy*
seven stars in the night
if the Baaka* stops flowin'
no-one gonna survive

from the sunrise
to the sunset
through the red dust
through the gumleaf smoke
we rise

the sunrise in the east
sun sets in the west
dance to my heartbeat
spirit in my chest

wanna see change, wanna see joy
wanna see pride, wanna be strong
wanna see heart, wanna see hope
wanna see dance, wanna hear song

I wanna feel rain on my face
I wanna feel sun on my skin
I wanna sit by the river
and feel the unity within

I wanna see a clean up
this country's part of me
needs harmony
my people call this river Baaka*
and it's like my artery

it's not hard to see
these opportunities that start with me
we represent our ancestors
this land of the Barkandji

---

* *see glossary pp. 165-172 for translations*

burnt out cars and broken glass
this country needs respect
my people sick, so clean this tip
check out and cash collect

protect our water
this disgrace to the human race
clean up this country, all the waste
we leave no trace

country is my medicine
country is my heartbeat «

** see glossary pp. 165-172 for translations*

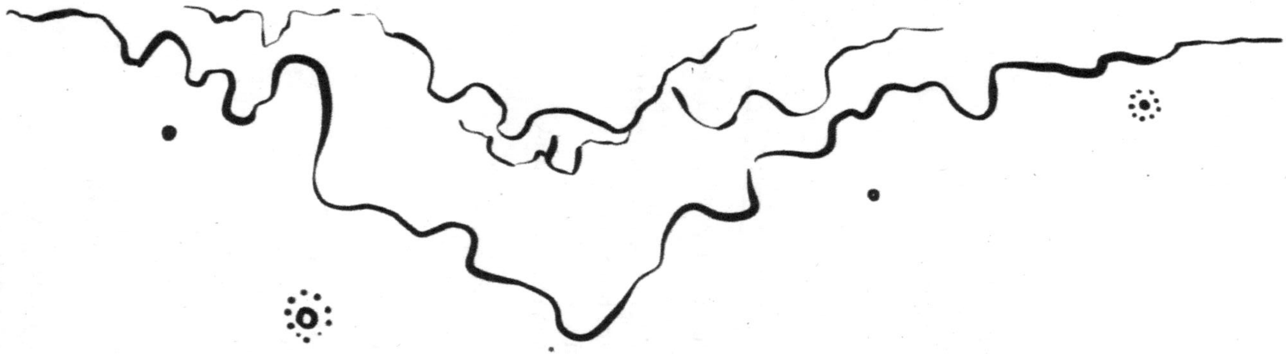

COUNTRY IS MY HEARTBEAT

WHERE THE EAGLE ROAMS

» COOMIE CREW

» we come from Coomealla
it's the Barkindji Crew
out in the bush we get in trouble
coz there's nothing to do

makin' our lives
into something brand new
we all stand tall
and there's nothing that you can do

belong to red dirt country
where the rivers meet
move your feet from Namatjira Avenue to Tapio Street
shake a leg on the backstreets
hot concrete, my black feet
show respect when the Elders speak

Pooncarie Settlement
to Coomie Mish
'tharlta' is kangaroo
'parntu' for fish
keep it tradish
my people at a standstill
massacre, trauma
buried at the sand hill

this my land still
and we still true
we still fight despite all of
the pain that we been through
the grief too
but brah, there's nothing we can't do
we black, strong and proud
get it through your thartu*

I go with – the sun and the moon
gotta follow my dreams – but I'll be back soon
where the eagle roams – that's where I go
follow ya ancestors – to get back home

everybody got a knife in the back
we all carry these bags of stone
I take one step forward then it's three steps back
remember that you're never alone

suicide is on my mind
it's taking up my time
this depression
kickin' in from behind

gotta stop this violence
gotta break this silence
but this anger and judgement
is clouding my mind

violence, disrespect, wanna run away
don't belong, don't really wanna connect
if I don't, I'm lost, I lose myself
I lose this culture I need to protect

get it into your head and stopping hating
no matter which opportunities, I'm takin', bred*
where my relations from the start of creation
come together ... we one nation ... yet? «

** see glossary pp. 165-172 for translations*

RIVER TO THE SEA

» 380 CREW

» my soul, the sun, the sand, the sea
I feel it washing over me, washing over me
connected to the Birrinbaa
fought, survived, we've come so far, come so far

this is where we live
on this sand we sit
this land's a gift
watchin' my family's spirit lift

we are grateful to exist
we are dancing in the mist
like our ancestors did
all of my mob raise your fist

there they were, jarjums* running free
listen to the knowledge passed to me
duraagan from the river to the sea
this is how it came to be
this is our identity
if you listen deep
you will hear the spirits speak

they said it would change when?
when will these days end?
they wanted us caged in
but we ain't gonna stay in!

they said it would change soon
but we ain't seen change yet
we singin' the same tune
my DNA is struggling to forget!

** see glossary pp. 165-172 for translations*

there's pain in these memories
there's trauma in my bloodline
there's power in my ancestry
this saltwater and sunshine

my Elders held this destiny
these rights and sacred sites
gonna redefine my history
and take darkness into light

my soul, the sun, the sand, the sea
I feel it washing over me, washing over me
connected to the Birrinbaa
fought, survived, we've come so far, come so far

to find the truth we gotta look inside
we're traumatised, we cannot lie
sit around by the campfire
it is in plain sight, and we can't hide

we gotta move forward
but at the same time
we know that this healing
is gonna take time
we know that this healing
is gonna take time

gotta be lookin' after my country
like my ancestors taught me
from the land to the sea
country speaks to me
through my song and story

if I'm looking after my country
then she's looking after me
cleansing my mind and my body
river to the sea
washing over me «

BREAKING HABITS

» GITHABUL NEXT GENERATION

» welcome to the place
where the bellbird song
means the sun settin' over
Muli Muli and Woodenbong

Yillingilly wahlu
this Githabul land
where five rivers start flowin'
that's where we stand

ayyye! what ya doin'?
nah nothing, playing tips
comin' straight outta Muli Muli
wiggle them hips

catch fish for dinner
swimming in the creek, bottom falls
make sure you get home
before the bellbird calls

Githabul people
reppin' these mountain ranges
like we've always done
for thousands of generations

connected to my tribal system
my mob
protecting my country coz
that's my job

I've got passion for knowledge
for wisdom of old
for the story of my country
that's still untold

Githabul
Gullabul
Narrakbul
Windjunbul
Wahlabul
my people stand strong together

my deadly aunties over Muli there
made a decision
seen the old fellas
resting up the back of the mission

see the tip gettin' bigger
running into the river
figure we need a new system
better flip the position

recycling's a mad trick
re-use some plastic
tap it together, and like magic
it's clap sticks
chuckin' a backflip
my cousin, the fact is
the system don't work
gotta try a new tactic

paper – that's trees
glass – that's sand
that means mines keep diggin'
and pollutin' my land

we gonna sort it, bin it
smash it, make it
me and my people
take a habit and break it

keep the cycle flowing
like back in old lore
without respect for nature
all nations will fall

work harder, stand tall
only got one earth,
help the land rebirth
yeah, country comes first «

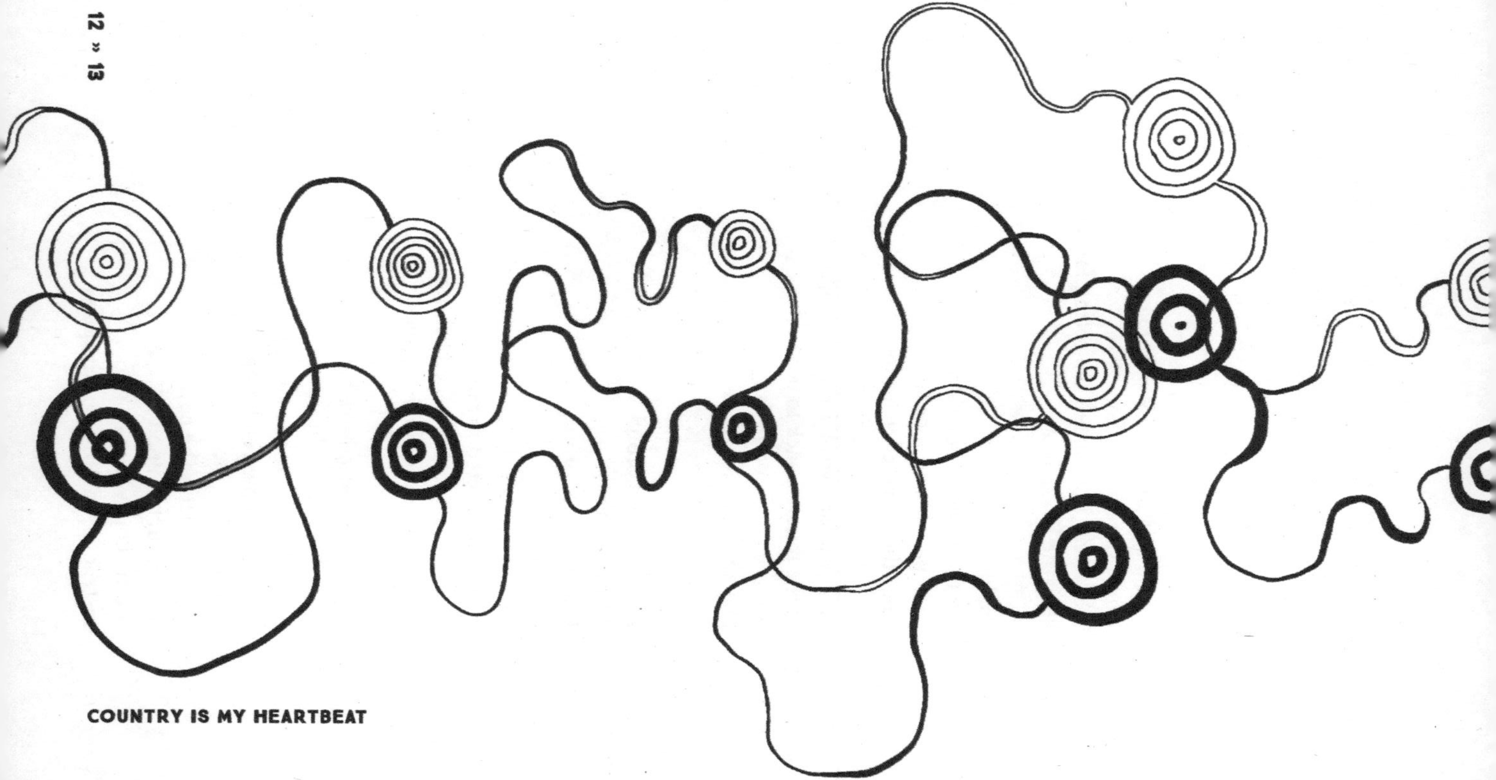

OUR COUNTRY, OUR WAY

» THE WILCANNIA MOB: INTERGENERATION

» ngai*, welcome to Wilcannia
where the Darling flow
starts near Bourke but the cotton farmers
keep the Paaka low

Paakantji Nation
ten thousand generations
been people of the river
since the dawn of creation

take you for a stroll from the Mally
to the mission back to town
warriors and boomerangs
play to shake the ground

wiimpatjas*
Paakantji and proud
wiimpatjas*
Paakantji and proud

river got sick
it's like it affected my mob
it's like my people ditched fishing
for smoking and sipping grog

my people started rowing
started pointing the bone
forgetting trauma's like a shadow
that will follow you home

well the past is the past
and enough is enough
hit the laneway to be safe
instead of walking past the pub

shake a leg in the red dirt
we dance in the dust
in waaku*, bilyara*, ngaatchi*
we trust

Paakantji – run like the wind
you know I'm going to prove you wrong
bit of courage and guts, hard work, determination
gotta protect our culture for the future generations

wiimpatjas* – run like the river
we keep our culture strong
got strength and respect flowing from my ancestors
on this land where we belong

kiira kiirinanha*
makwarra kilparra*
kiira kiirinanha*
Paakantji wiimpatja*

don't panic, get smarter
work harder, help yourself
going to make better choices
going to make better choices

keep your eyes on the prize
nuh never give up
being a leader for my people
takes courage and guts

so give it up for the Paakantji
Wilcannia's on the map
they reckon culture on the way out
we bringin' it back

** see glossary pp. 165-172 for translations*

people think we can't do it
but we givin' it a crack
can't forget about the colours
red, yellow and black

we back – we outsmart ya
us noongus* at the core
songline flip the script
kickin' down the door

sister girl spittin'
like ya never seen before
it's written in the stars
seven sisters brought the lore

born and bred Wilcannia, cuz
this is where we at
once you cross the Darling
we know you're comin' back

let me see them hands
if you feelin' the track
we Paakantji proud
yep we Paakantji black! «

** see glossary pp. 165-172 for translations*

DEEP SEA DREAMING

» BOWEN CONNECTION

» whichaway?*
let me tell you something
wattamooli!*
that's my introduction
Juru lan!
that's where we come from
South Sea to PNG!
fresh productions

trust it
since back in the day
ancestors painted on caves
muckin' about in the bay
foolin' around in the waves
when nothing was fake

settlement – FACT
affected our development – BLACK
took us out of our element – WHACK

now we tellin' it
spittin' a rap
bringin' it back
flippin' a track
Juru Nation
slavery on the plantation
plain to see
Stolen Generations
bravery
can't label me

we got the mangoes and mangroves
you don't really wanna tango like that though
come look for mud crabs, eso*
that's our lingo, now let's go!

family, mob, connect, support
that's our joint like Yasso point
asa fish trap
where we like to kick back – that's our choice

our spirit is alive and it will never die
we dancing on the beaches
through the changing of the seasons
got the sky, sand and the Deep Sea Dreaming

so all of my balas makin' a noise
we gonna set and deploy
play with the system like toys
rap for my people in need of a voice

I speak from the heart
I'm keepin' it real
if you from Bowen
then you know the deal
you know the feels
you know the reals
you need the skills
if you got the skills
you pay the bills

old world, new world
so many things change in this cruel world
and the truth it hurts
we can save the earth but we gotta do this first

** see glossary pp. 165-172 for translations*

you gotta go get you some
stop with the hate
and start with the love
you gotta know where you from
where you going, what you want
connection
trust

our spirit is alive and it will never die
we dancing on the beaches
through the changing of the seasons
got the sky, sand and the Deep Sea Dreaming «

DHINAWAN TOUCH THE STARS

» THE MOB

» my songline criss-cross
from coast to coast
stories of my culture
that we holding close

this the black soil plains
where the songline start
the story of my people
Dhinawan* up in the stars

this a call out
from the north to west
and if you know the emu dreaming yarn
y'all connected

to the black dirt
that's beneath ya feet
coming fresh outta Walgett
where the two rivers meet

couple cods
and a yellowbelly
couple Johnny cakes
have a yarn to Aunty
bit of conversation
this how we do it
in Kamileroi Nation
throw ya dubs up
reppin' all of my relations

** see glossary pp. 165-172 for translations*

you can feel it
round the campfire light
you can hear the clap sticks
when you close your eyes
get ya friends and ya family
and hold them tight
stay strong
we gonna be alright

my country where the songlines are
where Dhinawan* touch the stars
sunset, see the red light glow
my heart beats to get back home

we dealing with
the kinda stuff that'll get ya down
that stuff what ya do when ya bored
livin' in a small town
that sadness is all around us
yep, trauma and pain gets passed down, cuz
copy what ya mum and dad does
and what ya brothers do
it's my family and my friends
that I look up to
shapes my values
makes me who I am
a black superwoman
or a black superman

blackfella spray paint
on the back of your right hand
used to hold a spear
now ya holdin' a mic stand
used to follow lore
now ya follow the white man
used to read stars
now we follow the nav man, a black man

gotta read the signs ahead
choose the right path
got young fellas
lookin' up to you, bred*
watching your every step
every path you tread
every choice you make
you better make it your best

this is our time
it's time to make a choice
this a song for my people
stand up and raise your voice
this a message and it's special
for the little girls and boys
speak the truth
be fair dinkum and make some noise
pull yourself out of the drain
get up out of the gutter
continue the story
of your great great barji* and ya darthar*
show the love
and respect one another
don't let it go in one ear
and out the other
love ya, my dhagaan*
love ya, my brother «

** see glossary pp. 165-172 for translations*

LOOKING OUT FOR COUNTRY

» GITHABUL NEXT GENERATION

» taking it back to the olden days
Githabul country that's our place

where the sunshine over Mount Lindsay
in the mornings get them golden rays

it's home for us, it's home for you
we seen what the cows and pigs can do

lotta these species introduced
stopped our natives reproducing

used to be more water in the creek
waterholes were a lot more deep

day by day, week by week
that cycle's on repeat

listen when the Githabul people speak up
don't sit back and kick your feet up

this ain't no storm in a teacup
grab that mic, turn that beat up

when I'm looking out for country
country looks out for me
when I'm looking out for country
country looks out for me

what we gonna do, what's it gonna take
this is our home at stake

these Githabul People are standing strong
singing our country a brand new song

once ya dig it up, can't break it down
once introduced then stays around

metal and plastic – stuck with it
nobody gunna – come get it

well we sick of that waste – running amok
took two tonnes of it off in a truck

this stuff never comes down to luck
if it's ever gunna happen – it starts with us «

PMARA NURNAKA (GOOD COUNTRY)

» NTARIA CONNECT

» wurta pmara marra nurnaka*, Ntaria
nurna untharlaapuma, ngurrala*

culture is strong
we go for bush tucker
tjurnpaka – big goanna
ramiaka – sand goanna
kara-arraka – kangaroo
yirrampaka – honey ant

I see a new sunrise
our future is long
when I'm soaking in the sunshine
singing my song
spirit in my bloodline
my people are strong
wurta pmara marra nurnaka*
where I belong

where my country, culture
my skin
inside my spirit
imma find it within
don't fear it, feel it
and the strength it bring
teach it, share it
now let it begin

pmara marra nurnaka
nurna marra tnyinitjika
pmara marra nurnaka
arrkana kuta nitjina

our country is good
we have to look after our country
our country is good
be happy all the time

urrtjerrama
tell me the truth
drinking and fighting
kaaka* acting the fool
grief, ganja and grog
relha mapa* confused
relha mapa marra nitjika*
this song's for you

change gunna come
like rain gunna fall
like my spirit is strong
and it's written on the wall
it's written in the stars
wherever I go
we Western Arrarnta mob
now you know

this is my home
this is my truth
you wanna see change, huh?
it's over to you
I wanna see change, cuz
where do I go?
connect to your culture
and let everybody know «

---

see glossary pp. 165-172 for translations

HOMELAND CALLING

» THE LURRA COLLECTIVE

» Barlngadarr
Baraba, Lumbirra, Marlirri,
Wurrbarn, Wakmarran, Karrdbarn, Bularrdja, Naburrdo
Bunku, Warrdangu, Warragarrdi,
Bullumurr, Nadjodi
Gulmardu, Gurro, Mawalangu, Miridj,
Garadjangnu, Mowarlangu

homeland calling
wet season rain been falling
make the thunder and rain
old people walking
ancestors sharing knowledge
together

all my people from:
Ndjebbana
Kuninjku Burrara
Kunbarlung Na-kara
Kune Yolngu Matha
Wulaki, Dj'inang across this land
many many bungul*, many many clan
got many many songline, too many dance
ballinda*, binning*, now raise your hands
Yo, Maningridoh!

homeland calling
all my people singing along «

---

* *see glossary pp. 165-172 for translations*

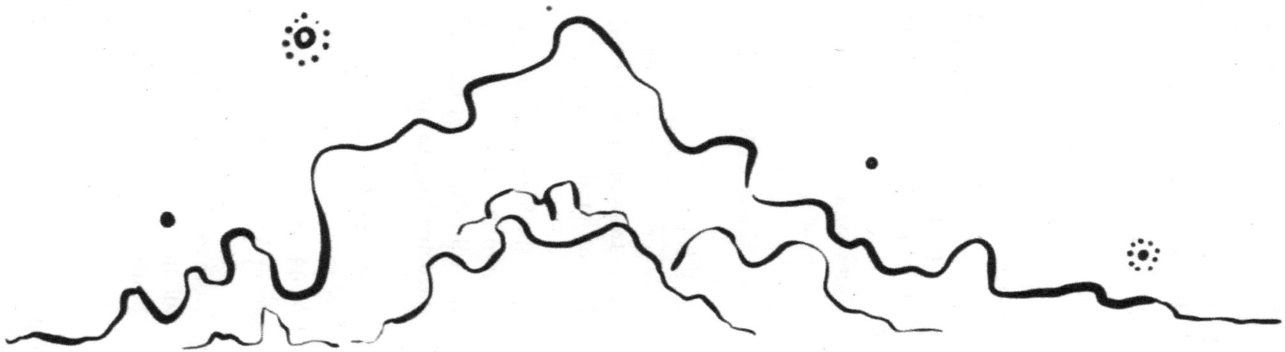

PEOPLE OF THE MOUNTAINS AND THE SEA

» THE BLACK DUCKS

» jarrambol
this country's where I come from
saltwater, sand
gudu* land where I belong

south coast yarn
gurrugama*, westerly wind
Monaro/Yuin
black country, black skin

let it begin
another track, another day
we're from the mountains to the sea
like the bundian way

from the fisheries, rock pool
quarantine bay
these little black ducks
got something to say

quack quack – nah, gammin'*, cuz
we're loud and proud
bring the bunna*, rain and thunder
all over the town

from the Stolen Generations
all the way to right now
destination, we've been waitin'
now we're wearing the crown

the first generation
the chain and whip
to 1967
black citizenship

we got invaded, misled
confused and frustrated
even though my people been here
since the earth was created

we are the people of the mountains and the sea

ain't nothing but a cutthroat world
that we livin' in
livin' on the mission or commission
never givin' in

Yuin and Monaro living here
in plain sight
but now the black flag flyin'
at the same height

doin' cuz, what's crackin'?
black ducks on the track
true fact is
that we ready to attack

bring it back, old ways
old culture and songs
like that old man
singing on the beach to Old Tom

** see glossary pp. 165-172 for translations*

we've come a long way
up the winding road
now the past is behind us
and we're ready to go

we're ready to grow
and we're letting you know
that we remember
and never ever letting it go

yo, we at the crossroads
make your choice
like my uncle said
"gudyuga*, raise your voice!"

bring the noise
yep, ready or not
"Where ya headed?"
where? what?

from the bottom
now straight to the top!

we are the people of the mountains and the sea «

** see glossary pp. 165-172 for translations*

PUUYA KUNTHA

» IRON RANGE DANGER GANG

» Lockhart is our ngaachi*
it's our homeland country
we them east coast Murris
we all have the courage
carry heaps of knowledge
we got plenty swimmin' holes
and waterfalls and our beaches gold
land is beautiful
it's colourful
like the water glow
hat nyakamu*

mepla* from Iron Range
where the rainforest meets the sea
my totem upan*, yawan*, muthuuy
pulu*, piwu*, iwayii*
Kanthanampoo, kuku yawu
Umpila, Wutathi
Kaanju*, Utha Langu*
mepla* danger for malkarri*

we go fishing, swimming, hunting
catching ream, barra, mullet
turtle, dugong, lubly
we go walkabout in the sunshine
tukulu* on the reef

** see glossary pp. 165-172 for translations*

we go flipping in river and creek
we cut laps we pump 'em beats
from malkara to Ilway streets

mepla* deadly, mepla* smart
mepla* puuya*
kuntha* AH
strong heart yawai*, cuz
mepla* had it from the start

mepla* deadly mepla* strong
mepla* culture living long
mepla* proud when singin' our songs
mepla* know where we belong

poison damper along the coastline laka
truth will set you free
my people live with trauma every day
like cyclone on repeat
old man wu'u*
mana laka* our time is running low
gotta learn 'em song and shake-a-leg
so my culture can grow

less phone reception
more connection
gotta come together
we gotta learn 'em lesson
that's our medicine
for them in depression
family gives us strength
and protection
gotta watch yathu*
stop getting arrested
leave a good impression
on our mob and section
so one day you may get selected
for something better
live a life of perfection

wepla danger malkarri*
kai kai (food)
kup murri (ground oven)
ngachi
mukamukana
Watchi wutathi, Nundah, Kuttini, Angkuna, Pin Pin,
  Packers (our places)
Pama mukamukana kalmana (*many people come*)
Wulpunyu mukamukana kalmana (*many children come*)
I be look all dempla (*them people*) walkabout
miiye wiiyke lake (*get food from this place*) «

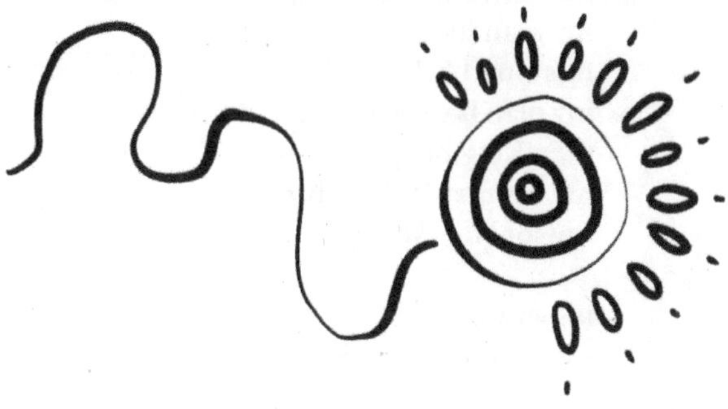

* *see glossary pp. 165-172 for translations*

ONE SONGLINE

» THE LÚRRA COLLECTIVE

» aw ngarrijah
ya njirramola good to see ya
borrarobjibba rdordbalk
pleased to meet ya
binning* bungul* mob
coming out ya loudspeaker
this be the Djomi* Djang
Maningrida

my grandfather, my teacher
my dance and my song
my grandmother, my leader
this land I belong
my plan is to be bigger and better
than King Kong
my country is my future
my songline strong

it's wrong
we got mining mob sniffin' around
where my soul and my spirit
sleep deep in the ground
you can hear the sound – KOH YEH
no messin' with my footprint – NO WAY
my mammam say – KOH YEH
and my mawa say – GO AWAY
all my people say – YOH WAY
can you feel the Maningrida mob – ALL DAY

one blood
one ceremony
one songline

a new day dawn day
breaks the night
singin' welcome to the future
imma be your tour guide
from the Ndjudda Point
to the new sub
connect to my country
that's true love

movin' up
OH YEH – got self-control
OH YEH – got a healthy soul
that's the way we roll
we shinin' brighter than gold
we share and come together
'round the yuyabol

my people walked the same footprint
for a long time
from a long line
back to right now
it's a new world
yet still steppin' on the same ground
look around, what do you see?
the future of my people is me «

** see glossary pp. 165-172 for translations*

WHERE I'M FROM

» BOOMALLI

» I'm from a place where the sun make ya dizzy
it's the home of the cod fish, long way from the city
I'm from a town where life can be tricky
where a brother go mad if he don't keep busy

I'm from a town
that can get a brother down
where a bottle and a bong
will leave ya six feet underground (that's right)

I'm from the Barwon
big river, big sky
twenty-eight thirty-three
they call it Collarenebri (Collarene-what?)

who's that?
another brother from the bush
be the first to back ya up
when shove come to push (I got your back, bra)

who's this?
another Murri from the mish
got an uncle named Eric
and he'll teach ya how to fish (let's go fishin')

who ya with?
damn right I'm with my brothers
if they rockin then we rollin
we ain't do it like the others (2833)

so check us out
nah no centrepoint tower though
no opera house
just the place where the flowers grow
country to the city
river to the beach
a lot of ground to cover
a lot to say to each

and everybody listen while I spit it
how I get it
Gomeroi Colly boy
they told me get it so I did it

hold up, let me think
I think I'm on to something
like how it feels when they sayin'
you won't amount to nothin'

and how it seems when you be down
and feelin' real under
but tryna figure shit out
got me thinkin' hard, I wonder

like what about the sacrifice?
what about the mothers who ain't here but still be with us,
right?
what about late nights recording, talking 3:05
just to give my people a sample and now we bangin' right

hate the feelin' when leavin'
but I gotta be strong
sad times even worse
got me feelin' so wrong

won't be gone very long
gotta do what I gotta
and when I get home
I promise I'll make it up, ma, I got ya

and it's on focus now don't trip, this is it
be legit about this shit get a grip
you only get one shot, one shot to be the man
so when I blow up you know that Colly made me who I am

I'm sayin' just remember though, it's 2833
and no matter where I be I put on for these streets
yo ... I said 2833
wherever I go, just know I'm throwin up the C like huh?

II

HISTORY IS IN MY BLOODLINE

WHAT WE CAN DO

» COWRA CREW

» yamma dumarung*
we the underdog!
on the Galari River
eagle on the rock!

fist in the air
for Erambie old people
who fought for years
for our mob

us blackfellas
know where we're from
gunna shake-a-leg
to our Dreamtime song

my people
kin
I'm proud and strong
from the country plains where I belong

my Elders from Eranbie Mission
started up the fight
self-determination, freedom
basic human rights

look at how far we've come
it's easier said than done
my kin fought with blood and fist
so we can dance beneath the sun

who are you?
know where you're from
know where you're going
who are you?
connection to your culture
will get you through it

my identity – you can't take it
my connection – you can't break it
my foundation – you can't shake it
look at this future we created

look at this situation since invasion
massacre, Stolen Generations
racist government, legislation
all across this sacred nation

it's no wonder my mob
keep getting caught up in this cycle
the Western way of thinking's gammin'*
like a downward spiral

you gotta remember your roots
they're pumpin' through your veins
bounce back, step up on that track
bringing it back to the ancient ways

gotta connect both the old and new
find a way, got to get us through
gotta get up, dust it off
show the world what blackfellas can do

** see glossary pp. 165-172 for translations*

how many acres?
thirty-two!
how many acres?
thirty-two!

gotta get up
dust if off
and show the world
what Cowra mob can do! «

TIME WILL TELL

» BWGCOLMAN MOB

» Munbara Bwgcolman burra
gubba*, the carpet python
head is magnetic
body is Palm Island
fine line between captain and crook
join the crew, take a tour round the history book

since my great grandfather was brought here in chains
1914, slavery with no wage
big shame – 1918 became a mission
PI became a prison – punishment by definition

nuh ya can't look forward if ya can't look back
gotta know the difference between lies and fact
the truth is beautiful, it's back and it's black
like the PI boys now we're ready to react

the Act – rewind to 1939
we think about home and family left behind as we rhyme
my words flow west across the sea line
connect to ancestors and the lessons of the Dreamtime

only time will tell
we no longer living under the bell
maybe change gonna come
like the morning sun
the Bwgcolman rise as one

2004 they were kicking down the door
Marshall squad held pregnant women to the floor
Elders, kids and all, what for?
telling lies in the court and the coroner's report

it's been a hundred years of trauma and fear
but the truth is the Bwgcolman warriors are still here
kicking back with another track, get it clear
speak out it'll make the pain disappear

we love this island
we sick of the silence
we can't change history
with crime and violence
we love this island
you can try to divide us
can't separate
forty plus tribes united

respect goes out to uncle Lex and the clan
the Bwgcolman people and the Doomadgee fam
the Tall Man got nothing on Munburra land
eeya lah, the Palm Island people taking a stand

only time will tell
we no longer living under the bell
maybe change gonna come
like the morning sun
the Bwgcolman rise as one «

---

* *see glossary pp. 165-172 for translations*

THE REAL WORLD

» CULTURE CONNECT

» welcome to Forbes, where the Lachlan River's fine
White Bend to Cottons Weir, where the waters intertwine
we survived the arrival, we alive, we tribal
on the mic we go viral, on your radio station

Stolen Generations, black and white separation
trying to make a difference – hard work and dedication
kids study at the school of hard knocks, learn the game
early smoke a little boof to escape, ease the pain

aye, cuz, what happened back in the day, I'll tell a story
  for ya
you can pass it down to ya son or ya daughter
till 1967 we were flora and fauna
now every single day my people dealin' with trauma

more funerals than holidays, no help and no guidance
comin' eighth in the state for domestic violence
driving with no license, ice and cop sirens
tired of living this life isolated in silence

yarning and sharing
changing our chemistry
back to what it's meant to be
black is my identity
people of the three rivers
we the survivors
we still alive
spread the word like wildfire

goin' fishing at Iron Bridge, swimming at White Bend
kayak and motorbike riding on the weekend
sitting down the river, kicking back, having fun
chucking backies off the bank, bruz enjoying the sun

wanna switch up the way my people think in this town
shake a leg on this ground, we proud and never
   backing down
on the track now, we need to stand up
DV stops with me – if you agree throw your hands up

you gotta walk the talk, if we raising our voices
we gotta back it up, brother, make the right choices
learn respect, learn it early, learn honesty
earn trust, learn it young, learn it properly

rapping and yarning and sharing with the mob
the whole community together, everybody get along
keep culture strong, my Elders past and present respected
the future's bright while my people connected «

STATE OF THE HEART

» DENI MOB

» forbidden from speaking our unwritten language
shifted into tin huts and given mission blankets
we made a living shearing but the town doors were closed
white flour, sugar, tea is not what we chose

our story is that thing
that lotta my people forgot
now it's all grog, drugs and cops
and my mob movin' around a lot
where that respect gone?
I'm black but I look white
where that respect gone?
connecting with that fire that burns inside

now it's all iPhone on the wifi
wanna connect but it's on the screen
not with your mob, never on country
but it's on the couch glued to the TV
step back and
we're from where the red gum grow
swamps and creeks where the Edward flow
we run these streets we search for freedom
under big skies where the red sun glow

I know when I'm wanted
and I know when I'm not
this sadness got me feeling
like someone this country forgot
but when I'm noticed
and acknowledged by my mob
that's when I know who I am
I know I belong

my mind frame changes
when I'm playing my part
it's not the shade of my skin
it's the state of my heart
I can't change who I am
this is all that I got
this is my mob, land and culture
and I'm keeping the lot

my mob is getting stronger
showing that you one of us
no more hiding round the campfire
in the smoke and the dust
better trust we your mob
this your country, this your song
this your story, this your river
this my mission, we belong

Hey, kooka*! – tell me some stories all 'bout what we used
to do
Hey, nyanka*! – tell us our history, sing us songs about
the truth
Kwe! – it's me, it's you, you're a part of this too
gotta take the ancestors' wisdom and we'll make it
brand new

never waste your time, never waste your mind, never
waste your ...
what?
potential
keeping things moving in a cycle
is fundamental
it's essential

** see glossary pp. 165-172 for translations*

keep your mental strong
keep the waste where it belongs
not on sacred country
move it along or use it later on

who's the most dangerous blackfella under the sun?
the most dangerous blackfella's an educated one «

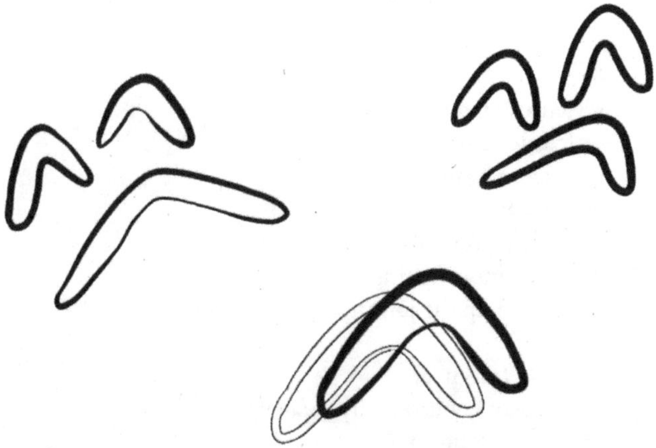

WHERE YA FROM?

» BOGGAMISH

» yaama*, Gomeroi dhawaan*
welcome to my country
my bawaa*, my dhagaan*
bagaay-gu*
where the Macintyre flow
with my mob, fishing
whipping up the johnny cake dough

what ya totem is?
Dhinawan*, yuutendaly*, yabaa*
forced onto stations
Kunopia, Welltown, Euraba
My great great great great grandfather
Old Toomelah
Bogga Mish movie star

keep it movin', brah
like a shooting star
let me hear ya say 'Boggabilla Toomelah'
Bogga Mish
droppin' this Boggabilla toomelah
mission manager rolled up
snakes all round
lost language
and culture on sacred ground
back on the mission
on the ration system
wanna learn your culture
gotta listen

minyaaya dhaay
nginda dhuura-nhi
where ya from?
minyaaya dhaay
nginda dhuura-nhi
where ya from?

I never knew that being black was a crime
'til I went up town and got sent to the back of the line
always coming in last
so we afraid to ask
getting told to get over the past
First people but we second class
you're invited to unlearn what you been taught
what you always thought
we need to talk about a bit more support
we need to talking about moving up
making change
if we never come together
then things stay the same
put ya head in the game
we all gammin'* and shame

Bogga Mish – let 'em know
bring back the old ways
brrrr brr brrr aye aye
bring back the old ways
racism ain't nothing new to me or to my community
my old people fought for opportunity
T.R.U.S.T.
check out the moves that we bust
keep our culture strong, we must
yaama*, ngingdaay gomeroi, cuz «

** see glossary pp. 165-172 for translations*

ABORIGINAL JUSTICE

» THE P.I. BOYZ

» well it's the P.I. Boyz
from Palm Island
kickin' back with another track
like the bullyman* sirens
the courts still lying
my people still dying
get your heads up, brother
P.I. Boyz are arriving

Black brother Morry
and we're taking it back
to the days when
they never even heard of rap
think back to the time
of the great kidnap
coz this the next level
and we ready to react

yo back in the day
this was paradise
we were living off rations
like a bag of rice
we never got paid
but we paid the price
my culture faded away
like day to night

but we stayed alive
and we still right here
we the Bwgcolman tribe
and it's the end of your career
no fear
because we ready to drop
it's the boys from Palm Island
we the head of hip hop!

listen up everybody
they call me Patch
you hear me ripping up a CD
and I'm letting it scratch
it's true what they say
the boys are back
get up off your chair
and get ready to clap

so the pub closed down
and we smuggle the grog
and it's alcohol
that troubles the mob
brawling on the streets
so they doubled the cops
who else is going to rap
if we decided to stop

straight to the top
nuh nothing has changed
from Doctor Point all the way back
to Cootes Lane
since my great grandfather
was brought here in chains
yeah I'm writing this rap
so you remember his name

** see glossary pp. 165-172 for translations*

this is for my brother
that was taken away
from his family
I wish he was alive today
we're looking for justice
Aboriginal way
not just locking up my mob
for starting a fray

yeah it starts today
nup, no more of this
listen to the words
scratched on this disk
tale of paradise
and the way we lived
we got the past and the present
look at all of this «

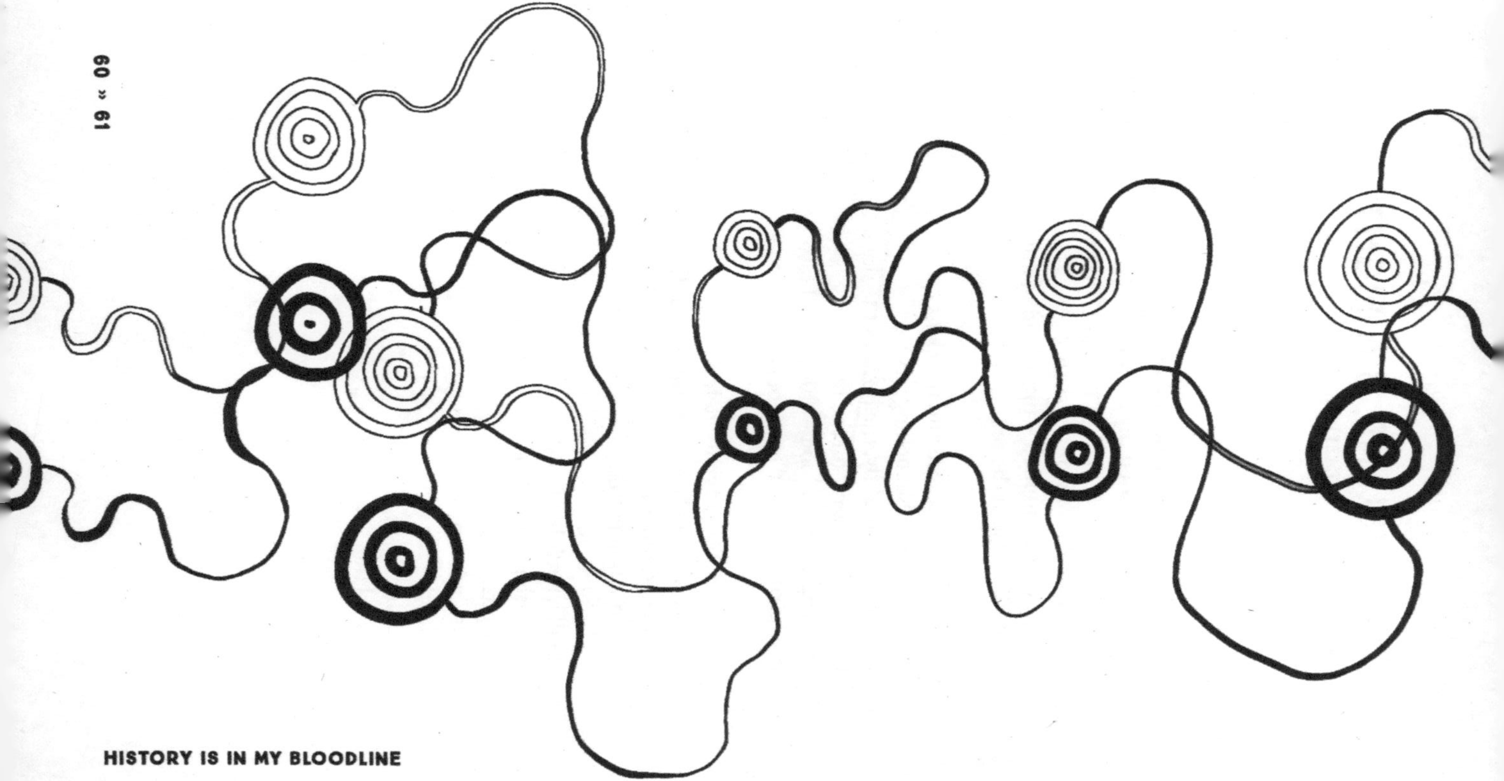

SMALL ISLAND, BIG FIGHT

» IRWARPAUP FT. TAMYOK

» we wrote you a rhyme about way before time
when Gelam created my island
he sailed the seas on a strong sager* breeze
and created a song out of silence
two islands combined – this island of mine
a paradise lost in the sea

Malo created the lore and the clans
and the totem that belongs to me
the creatures that fly, the birds in the sky
the fishes that dive on the reef
my people – my blood – this island I love
my spirit – my soul – my belief

warrior nation zogo le* defend
respect the Meriam clans, understand?
tag maukie maukie*
teter maukie maukie*

small island, big fight!
small island, big fight!
my spirit – my soul
my island – my fight
my land – my right
small island, big fight!
small island, big fight!

since beginning begun
my roots, my clan
my straight up – island way
my warriors fought on the sand in the sun
and I speak recognition today

1981 – a Meriam man lodged a claim to say
Mabo and others and sisters and brothers and mothers
would ignite the flame
the flame would burn, the world would learn
you can't take my island away

tag maukie maukie*
teter maukie maukie*
the spirits protecting his grave

we dream to succeed, achieve, believe
the future's right in front of me
now is the time for my island to shine
a paradise lost in the sea

from person to person for ages to come
from Koiki my legacy be
my island
my dream
the future is you
and it's me «

** see glossary pp. 165-172 for translations*

THE WILD MID-WEST

» MULLY MOB

» I'd like to welcome you to Mully
in the wild midwest
Mully wha? Mullewa?
Mullewa! Yes!
wanna hear my story?
be my guest
my black brother
is comin' up next

well it's hard to accept
what happened in the past
from the bush to the Common'
it was hard from the start
not allowed in town after dark
not allowed in the shops
or the pool or the bar

it was written in the stars
it was written in the sand
it was written on the wall
it was written by hand
by the black man
this is our culture
this is our land
gotta listen if you wanna understand
it's a new generation
it's a new day
if you work
then you gotta get paid
no more slaves
coz we're living two ways
whitefella, blackfella
should be treated the same

Mullewa – doesn't matter who you are
doesn't doesn't doesn't matter who you are
Mullewa – doesn't matter who you are
gotta reach up for the stars

Mullewa – doesn't matter who you are
doesn't matter who you are
gotta be up for the task
gotta learn from the past
be proud of who you are
gotta get down on the track
put Mully on the map
proud of my culture
we bringin' it back
sing it out loud, proud and black
gunna rap it out
Mullewa's where it's at

gotta be strong, getting ready for the game
gotta be proud, no time to be shame
this is life in the fast lane
getting ready for the rain
no pain, no gain «

BUILT TO LAST

» CAIRNS MURRI CREW

» beautiful ... welcome to Cairns
the tropical gateway to North Queensland
beautiful ... you can take it from me
summer heat, palm trees, beach, reef and Daintree
beautiful ... and it sounds so sweet
tweet of lorikeet, bare feet on Murri Street
a three-day trip can turn in to three weeks
sunshine, blue sea, tight rhymes and dope beats

it wasn't always easy
it wasn't always paradise
my old people fought hard for land rights
there wasn't any opportunity
freedom for my community
old people treated brutally
nothing you can do can break our spirit

we build to last
so stomp with me
sand beneath my feet
now hear my people speak
dance to the rhythm of your heartbeat

it took a little bit of time from arrival
to get our non-white history even taught up in high school
once lookin' down the sights of a rifle
now celebratin' our culture and survival
haters – like spiteful
I break cycles
why?
this attitude has gotta change
it's not about black and white
or about stereotypes
just people being treated the same

check it out, we on track
we ready to attack it
break the cycle
like you break a bad habit
if you ever get an opportunity
you gotta grab it
coz our great grandfather
never ever had it

I can tell ya, bro – If you don't know where you been ...
I can tell ya, sis – If you missed out on your dreams ...
I can tell you that the spirit is strong, and if you know
the song
then you can sing along with me «

MY GENERATION

» B-TOWN WARRIORS

» calling on my generation
calling all my people, my relations
singing with the wind of four nations
songlines of the first creation

we from the north to the south
to east to the west
four winds, four tribes
one country what we represent
Bourke cousin
yep we showing respect
ancestors, old people
that we laid to rest

massacre at Myall creek
living on wild meat
Corroboree at Innaminka
dancing in bare feet
from the mission in Bre*
started working at thirteen
sun-up to sundown
in forty degrees
for free

in '67 white man
gave us the vote
even though the same white man
came here on a boat
what a joke!
they even tried to take the lingo we spoke
but they didn't know
our spirit spinning in the gum leaf smoke

learn my story
and my song
and my tradition
from the past
sitting round the campfire
listening yarns
keeping it real
keeping it going from the start
story of my ancestors
written in the stars

my generation
got addicted to the screen
forgot my connection
got my Dreaming from TV
it's like we lost hope
swapped it for grog and dope
grief, loss and trauma
like a slippery slope
don't forget what you are worth
you gotta take pride in the place of your birth
despite all the trouble and hurt
you represent the oldest culture on earth

to keep it real you got to:
take your time to listen to old people and
strengthen your mind
you gotta walk along the rivers and creeks in bare feet
coz the truth is in my country is me
this is something you can never ignore
respect for your own self coz that's sacred lore

** see glossary pp. 165-172 for translations*

so stay black with a swagger
and keep it in step
coz BT Dub on the mic
and the future's looking better, yep
we stick together ready set
we connected looking fresh
while there's breath in my chest
then my culture's never dead «

TIME WAIT FOR NO-ONE

» ILAN STYLEZ

» wiswei*, bala*, sissy?
kassa, wanna know
where youpla from?
where the oobarr* grow

me Zenadth Kes got their wires crossed
and now Zenadth Kes becomes paradise lost
ina noomunlag* surrounded by athabad*
murra kazil*, lagau kab*
Zenadth kes diew gassoman*
mepla* baptal tookoi pal
coming up to run amuck
iy pu nagamik we love it
laka every one of us

mepla* lived in harmony for generations
Island Nations of the Torres Strait
and then the white man arrived in paradise
and took my island lifestyle away

yawor now, wati-siga, grog
shamejob, you mob
not mepla* culture
when's it gonna change
dopey in the head
dim diem, walking dead
like a zombie, sirip-em
when we gunna be the same?

** see glossary pp. 165-172 for translations*

time wait for no-one
flow like the ocean
like poetry in motion
steady steady coasting
riding on the tides just floating
cruise on the coastline
steady steady coasting
steady steady coasting

mepla* warrior people we be living by the sea
it's who you were, who you are
who you continue to be (free)
issa blessing not a curse, our diversity
you see, you be you, I be me perfectly

music's number 1 effect is to connect
me altogether larn you apasin respect
like something in the water we reflect upon the depth
teach 'em bout our culture and our country and the rest

you feel it in your body when you're dancing it's the best
assa rhythm of our heart that's beating
deep within our chest
4 winds on my back, north, south, east, west
dressed to impress nonetheless our interest
is to project what we want to protect «

** see glossary pp. 165-172 for translations*

YAEGL BIIRRINBA

» 380 CREW

» we are the saltwater people FRESH
ginagaay* check my label
some Bundjalung some Gumbaangir mob YES
everyday reppin' the Yaegl willing and able

listen up rip it up, brah SHH
get ready don't hate just ninginaa*
we are the saltwater people YES
waanji* singin' up Biirimbah

Yaegl mob
yep still surviving
yambora back
to Ullagundi Island
we risen
we rising
like sun on horizon
they been telling us lies
yet while I'm alive
my culture never be dying

my Elders had the resilience
they had it from the start
they got massacred by the millions
history makes us who we are
our hearts are shining with brilliance
the mystery's in the stars
this whole time we've been feeling it
now I'm ready to play my part

** see glossary pp. 165-172 for translations*

telegraph to the street corner
drew an invisible line
segregation, isolation
limitations in their mind
then came demonstration
1965 the Freedom Rides
now it's my relation
Yaegl Nation, and we regaining our pride

ginagaay* dyinda*, gagu*
Yaygirr Nya Yundi
ginagaay* dyinda*, gagu*
Yaegl Biirrinba*

our Dreaming might be from a time of old
but look around
it's everywhere
it can't be bought
or sold
it's sacred ground
flows from the mountains
down the valley
and runs into the sea
created by Dharaagan
and that's how it came to be
reminiscing on the Stolen Generations
back in the day
gubbas*, mission manager
takin' all the children away
now it's opportunity, education
now look how times have changed
all the complications throughout the ages
old people paved the way
I'll shape my own identity
I'm just the way I'm meant to be
it's in my blood
my destiny
gotta show the whole world
the best of me
our hearts are in this sacred land
connection to my race and fam

direction
yep that greater plan
respect for all of my Yaegl clan
culture's cycle
just keeps on going
'round the campfire
learning, growing
learn who I am
at the deepest knowing
like the ol' Birrimbah
keeps on flowing «

** see glossary pp. 165-172 for translations*

DJABUGANYDJI BAMA

» KDA CREW

» welcome to Kuranda
where the beat drops in the treetops
where we rock with green tree frogs
and the gunyarra*, them big crocs

this is hip-hop from Kuranda
where the Barron meets the sea
where we smell curry and campfire
get ready for a big mad feed

cultures in my veins
my history's in my bloodline
this knowledge is in my brain
my story's within my songline
keep our culture alive
guri buga djunal* – one time
young and bright in the streets
light and sunshine

we them deadly bama ngungi*
coming up from Djabugay country
ya, Indigenous mob

yabbas*, djidgas*, bunjis*, murris*
home of the

budajjii*, guyi, bundarra*
our creator
bullurru*, dulbil*, gangla*, djama*, gunyarra*

bringin' this culture
back on the track
we Djabugay – BLACK
reggae – RAP
KDA, him again?
TG, can't get much better than that!
with my family at my side
strong love that you can't hide, see?
you can't deny that strength that I get
with my ancestors behind me

Bulmba bulurru
Boonda bana wurru
Budajji bundarra*
bama ngungi* Tjunburru

we got fighting on the streets
my people dropping like leaves
better believe this grog and ganja
come from trauma and grief
what's beneath? where the relief?
we got too much pressure to measure
all the mob from four communities
gotta come back together

anxiety and depression
inside of me got me stressing
sometimes and second guessing
and fighting my self-expression
now listen to the definition
'what ya missin' on this mission!'
we can lessen the stress
if we learn one simple lesson
and stick together forever

** see glossary pp. 165-172 for translations*

harmony in our community
unity for you and me
education is truly key
if it is truth you seek
people stream on screens
but we believe in dreaming by creeks and greenery
don't be a scheming demon
we beamin' peace in this scenery

opportunity, strong community
gotta go make that change
because you can heal yourself
you can heal yourself from that pain
that shame
you can break that chain
you gotta lift your game
you gotta grab that mic
sing your song
'til everybody shout your name «

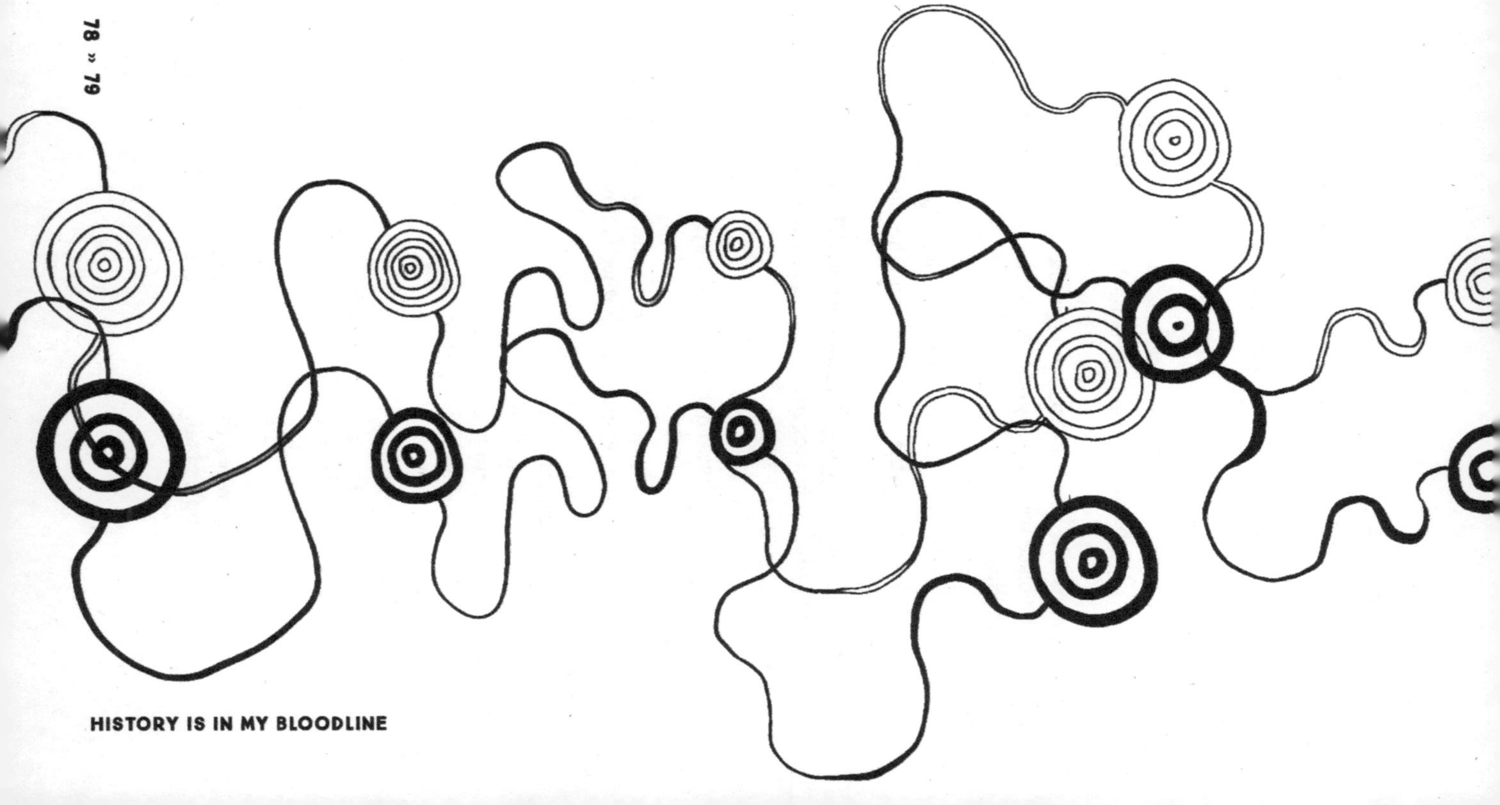

CALLING INTO THE DEEP

» 380 CREW

» let us take you back – I can see the scene in a vision
the past, present, future of Ngullagundahgi Mission

let us take you back to Ngullagundahgi Island
the place we put our pride in – where children always
smiling

let us take you back – to where we belong
where the branches reach high and the roots remain strong

let us take you back – we all mob, we all one
my people stand together – sand, saltwater and sun

let us take you back to 1961
tides rise and lives change and old ways undone

let us take you back to Pippi Beach and Hillcrest
where memories were made that we will never forget

our ancestors talk to us
yeah they walk with us
guiding us on our path
telling us 'darkness ain't gunna last'

calling into the deep
brings you out
darkness into light
love will get you through

life changed when the white man first came
and my people's pain is like the worst migraine

disconnect from my country and searching for fame
alive online and dead to my real name

so where you at?
you gotta make time to take time

bring it back
keeping the old ways alive

close your eyes and let the noise die down
love will get you through

old people like old trees that fed and nurtured
we go deep – these roots buried beneath the surface

reaching down deep – finding our real purpose
telling the real-time story of a dream serpent «

III | FLAME IN THE STRUGGLE

BRING IT BACK

» 2820 CREW

» let me take you on a journey
way back before
when the white man landed
on these sacred shores

settled our land
killed to build their walls
lest we forget the fallen
in the frontier wars

murder and massacre
pillage and rape
assimilation of my mob
was a big mistake

Nanima Mission
the first in the state
the spirit of my people's
something you'll never take

now mob think you're gwaani*
when you're doing it tough
good help is hard to find
when ya struggle to trust

my own people call wonga*
very quick to judge
don't forget
nobody below and nobody above

ya too shame to seek help
you only hurting yourself
one in three people struggle
with their mental health

Young Alyawarr men in Ampilatwatja, Northern Territory prepare for ceremony (Photo: Toby Finlayson)

This country. These connections. Freedom. Condobolin, New South Wales. (Photo: Josh Nicholas)

Young Wiradjuri man performs in 'Who I Am' by The Condo Crew, Condobolin, New South Wales (Photo: Toby Finlayson)

Ancient waterfall, fringing stone country, Maningrida, Northern Territory (Photo: Toby Finlayson)

Victor Rostron – songman and cultural leader, Maningrida, Northern Territory (Photo: Toby Finlayson)

Fist up for the B-Town Warriors – music video for 'Thundercloud' (Photo: Toby Finlayson)

Campfire yarns with the B-Town Warriors. Bourke, New South Wales (Photo: Toby Finlayson)

Fred Leone, Desert Pea Media facilitator and 2018 Board Member. Bourke, New South Wales (Photo: Toby Finlayson)

Drought country. Red dirt. Walgett, New South Wales (Photo: Nicky Akehurst)

'Kup Kar' on Thursday Island for 'Two Worlds' by Tagai Buway. (Photo: Toby Finlayson)

Toby Finlayson and B-Town Warriors shoot 'Dreams'.
Bourke, New South Wales (Photo: Nicky Akehurst)

Our brother. RIP. Millikapiti, Tiwi Islands
(Photo: Toby Finlayson)

Young Githabul legends in Woodenbong, New South Wales (Photo: Holly Robinson)

B-Town Warriors perform 'Dreams'. Bourke, New South Wales (Photo: Nicky Akehurst)

Mob from Cairns, Queensland on location (Photo: Toby Finlayson)

Owen Whyman Snr plays yidaki on Barkindji country. Wilcannia, New South Wales (Photo: Toby Finlayson)

Domestic violence awareness project. Broken Hill, New South Wales (Photo: Nicky Akehurst)

Campfire steez with the B-Town Warriors. Bourke, New South Wales (Photo by Toby Finlayson)

'Rissole' the emu, on location. Wilcannia, New South Wales (Photo: Toby Finlayson)

B-Town Warriors perform 'Dreams'. Bourke, New South Wales (Photo: Toby Finlayson)

nobody wanna talk about it
keep it on the shelf
in the meantime
my people keep killing themselves

wa-loo-win, wa-loo-win, wa-loo-win
bu-ga-ray-bung-ba-lung
   bring it back, bring it back, bring it back
   living black, my people bring it back

goo–ba–bee, gil–lee-ga, me-me-boo
gum-bung, ga-lung
   bring it back, bring it back, bring it back
   living black, my people bring it back

cruisin' down the mish
in my commodore
slappin' on the ochre
boondi* on the floor
survived genocide
Wiradjuri to the core
and if ya havin' trouble, cuz
you can give me call

you ain't heavy, you my budda*
you ain't heavy, you my sis
if I had to
I'd carry every person on the mish

you my mob, you ain't gwaani*
you ain't wonga*, ya crook
get ya health sorted
hit that illness with a left hook

** see glossary pp. 165-172 for translations*

Yal-bilinya yindyamarra*
learn respect
the future's in the past
and we need to reflect

connect, resurrect
let the new day begin
ancestors within the ochre
painted on my skin

since the first sun-up, cuz
my culture been strong
along the Wambool River
where my people belong

this song goes out to
all my loved ones and fam
strength comes from culture
connection to the land «

** see glossary pp. 165-172 for translations*

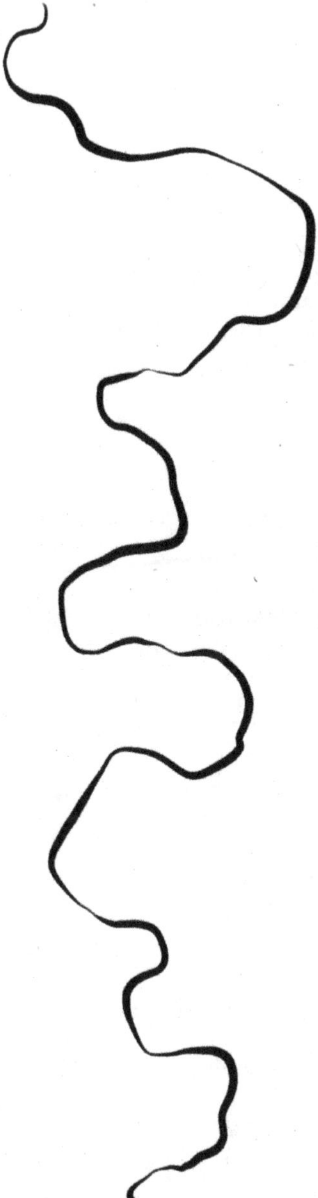

SPEAK WITH ME

» THE MOB

» consider this an invitation from the Walgett Nation

you want to speak with me?
'round the campfire is where we'll be
we'll take some space to breathe
I'll get to know you
and you'll get to know me
we're talking unity
under the gum trees
under the gum trees
we're talking unity

you could say
that we're thinking back
it's the ancient mob out of the gate
with a new track
yulligi yugul* on a boom bap
dance in the dirt
grip that mic
fade to black

never gammin'* gully
speak the truth
lotta trouble
lotta struggle
lotta mob got a short fuse
lotta confusion
mob getting left behind
lotta suicide
bruised on the inside
lotta rain
lotta thunder
mob won't go to the doctor
mob getting drunk

and going womba*
how much longer
'til ya get up
and get stronger?

I reckon it's a funny thing
whitefellas keep tipping that money in
but it don't seem to change a bit
things keep getting worse from where I sit
whitefella worker hard to trust, hard to cope
don't know this mob from a bar of soap
wanna put me under their microscope
no wonder me peeps keep losing hope

the skies are turning grey
it's dark and sad and broken
don't hide your spirit away
make sure your words are spoken
say what you wanted to say
my people barely coping
how we s'posed to focus
when it's hopeless
and the doors ain't open

step into my office, brah
down by the riverside
here's my card
it's not that tricky
it's not that hard
kickin' back around the campfire
heart to heart

** see glossary pp. 165-172 for translations*

step into my office, sis
Namoi Village or Gingi Mish
kick it to the river
might catch a fish
prove different cultures can co-exist

seems both sides
gotta learn to speak
to one another
my brother, don't turn ya cheek
gather round, listen up now
stomp ya feet
bangin' clap sticks
over that reggae beat

guwali, winangali – speak, listen, know
winangali diyamali – lift up «

HOW YA FEELIN'

» THE CONDO CREW

» now come on you kids
sit down around the fire
let's have a yarn
we need to talk about
what's goin' on for you young ones

truth is, it's hard
when you feel like you're down and out
go'n then
tell us what you got to be proud about
mob
family
land
songline
our lingo and lore here
since the Dreamtime

REWIND – remember back to your roots
rollin' barefoot, walking about with no boots
REWIND – back to when the sky was your roof
'round the campfire, yarnin' up, spittin' the truth
don't put yourself on mute
my name's Hope and I'm living proof
Condo youth will give you
something to listen to
on a mission to speak up
keep turning them beats up
we slither to the river when it heats up

hold up
watching two worlds collide

so what we gunna do about youth suicide

I think we need to connect
connect to what?
mob, culture that we need to protect

how ya feelin'?
are ya feeling down and out?
runnin' in a circle
stuck in a roundabout
stuck in the system
stop, look and listen
our mission
if there's a problem
we gunna fix it

I think it's my time to shine
I got a lot of questions
that are playing on my mind
like depression, trauma
the grief and the crime
all this negativity
we need to leave behind
kids doin' time
don't get caught in the trap
keep an eye on the youth
get your crew back on track
so listen to the facts
and follow your own map
while we stand on our land
coz we're proud to be black

sometimes you might feel like
you're in it alone
in the zone
no-one to turn to
just sittin' at home
sometimes you get shame
of people talkin' behind ya back
remember you deadly
reconnect, rewind the track «

CHANGES

» WAMBOOL WORLDWIDE

» welcome my mob, my brother, my tidda*
Wiradjuri country, Wombool River
kicking it, ripping it
keepin' this rhythmic
check this flow
we spitting like tiddelick

'boom' in my language, cousin
means Jurra
pay respect
show yindyamarra*
keep it gentle, rollin' slowly
honour the spirits that hold me

Bx bruz that's where we at
we from many nations proud and black
Walgett to Brie, yep round the traps
Cowra, Coonamble get down with that
history you can't ignore
massacre, murder, martial law
Windradyne 1824
it's time my people evened the score

** see glossary pp. 165-172 for translations*

grief and trauma's in my blood
mental health and suicide, bud
depressed and pressing, pokies, pubs
self-medicate with grog and drugs
loss of cultural identity
missed that songline, lost that melody
my people still search for that remedy
look in the mirror, your own worst enemy

my spirit and my soul
my people lost control
the pain will take hold
will take its toll
until you open your heart
no you can't change
if you don't start

strength in my roots
hope in the wind
strength in my soul
in the spirit within

couple of things we gotta explain
bit of knowledge you gotta obtain
I admit it – might sound strange
but ya stomach is your second brain
break it down, budda* boy
let's get technical
break it down, tidda* girl
teach me the medical
bush tucker food
very accessible
diet can level
your mental chemicals
make better choices
live your life
know your vibe
attracts your tribe
get more sleep and exercise
we gonna feel alright

yep, the future's looking brighter
the pressure's feeling lighter
make better choices
gotta release the spirit that's inside ya
strong enough
to live every single day
don't do work
but I still get paid
gotta lotta life to live
I admit that
if ya fall down
ya get right back up
and ya start being happy
don't act crappy
I love life and you should too
that's comin' from a kid that dreamt he flew «

** see glossary pp. 165-172 for translations*

PEOPLE OF THE RED SUNSET

» B-TOWN WARRIORS

» straight out of Bourke
where the Darling River's deep
where the Wonkamurra, Paakantji
Nyaampa, Murrawarri meet
connected to my country
red dirt through my black feet
can't track me
no guns but the sun packin' heat

I tell you it's hard
violence leaving scars
leavin' bruises, broken families
broken homes and broken hearts
smoking dope and getting drunk
skippin' school and stealin' cars
that type of yarn will get you nowhere
but behind bars
I'm sick of this misery
my culture like a mystery
massacre, Stolen Generations
up in my history
listen to this
with boomerang and clap sticks
you can hear it rockin' from up Northy
down to the Rizz

kids pickin' up bumpers LAH
drinkin', killin' your liver BRAH
better switch this up, better go to school
ya foolish think this cool or WHA
better raise them voices up
better make better choices YA
better respect, better keep in check
myself, my song, my culture HA

we from a place where the warm wind blows
my place, my home, my spirit
we the people of the red sunset
we connect like the flows in the river

better learn about myself
help my family's mental health
better check if you alright
better make sure that you sleep at night
better keep that dream alive
exercise and eatin' right
now's the time to show our pride
and take this yarn Australia wide

change it back to what it meant to be
I'll take back my identity
I'll maintain my integrity
I'm black in the twenty-first century

yep, there's still room for improvement
work with us to start a movement
Bourke about to change the game
and break the chain through this music

if you fair dinkum prove it, bred*
you better shake your leg
if you for real, sis
hands up if you feel this

if you on track
you better learn your lingo
bringin' it back
learn the facts
learn your language
yep, be proud, be black

** see glossary pp. 165-172 for translations*

we livin' black and white
get rid of that stereotype
never give up, don't quit
the truth is you can be anything you like
gotta grab that mic
gotta keep that fire alight
gotta keep on dreaming
keep your chin up
keep on shining bright «

THUNDERCLOUD

» B-TOWN WARRIORS

» this song is dedicated to
everyone who is struggling
no matter who you are
where you come from
what colour you is
keep ya chin up, cuz
you not in it alone

the weight of the world
feels like it's holding me down
I can't breathe, I can't eat, I can't sleep
blood pumping head to my feet
giving me a double heartbeat

the pressure and the pain
feels like a thundercloud
I'm underwater bubbling
I'm struggling to stand
but I'm stumbling, tumbling
trying to get to dry land

lately I been struggling
I been losing sleep
days turn into nights
nights turn into weeks
can't think, can't eat
nightmares on repeat
it's like the fire's going out
on these B-Town streets
thoughts run deep
wasn't always like this
is this really supposed to be
the way that life is?
take every opportunity

even though you might miss
coz my spirit runs deep
grip it with a tight fist

lately it's been hard
got plenty going on
no-one understands me
like I'm always in the wrong
trying to keep it altogether
tell myself to be strong
but at school, or home with mob
it's like there's nowhere I belong

another day, another drama
another funeral come around
grief
like an everyday yarn in B-Town
everybody getting locked up
they drunk and they stoned
and to top it all off
I got no credit on my damn phone

feel the weight of the world
feel the pressure and the pain
sick of doubt, sick of lame
sick of drama, sick of pain
gunna change this up
coz we the BT DUB
we be the leaders of a new age
new day – wassup?

don't doubt yourself
gotta be bigger, gotta be better
gotta be strong – get up!
we gunna give in? NEVER!
better pick yourself up
better make the right call

because together we rise up
and divided we fall

gotta lead by example, laysh*
gotta walk the walk
I never ever thought
people'd listen when I talk
now I'm focusing on sport
trying to stay away from court
I'll be the black brother that you need
when you're looking for support

don't let the pressure get you down
let the stresses of the town
pull a brother underwater
feeling like he 'bout to drown
take a different track
bring it back, feet upon the ground
all my brothers chin up
don't let the world get you down «

---

see glossary pp. 165-172 for translations

REWRITE YOUR STORY

» B-TOWN WARRIORS

» well I'm right, me Unc
coz I'm a Bourke breed reppin' this
gifted young poet
yeah my pen is where my weapon is
ready for the lesson, kids?
where ya self-expression is?
Lorla's on the mic again
careful who ya messin' with!

keep it on the low
maybe cruise around the levy, bred*
crank them vibes
and hit the pillow with a heavy head
stressed out
one out
nobody understands me yet
nobody got my back
so then myself is who I represent

check it
B-Town blessed with the method
Darling River tiddas*
and our word is our weapon
reppin' all the black people of Bourke
through all the trouble and the struggle
we still making it work

** see glossary pp. 165-172 for translations*

this a call out
to all my mob stuck in the room
we gotta sort out
whatever been making ya blue
we goin' all out
the Bourke mob
me and my crew
because you never alone
despite whatever you going through

never forget it's never too late
when it's dark and the sky is falling
get up and rewrite your story
trust that the sun will rise in the morning

I been connecting with my friend
now I'm feeling like myself again
it's freaky when you trust someone
you don't need to pretend
when somebody showing you
they know what you're going through
it's like a breath of fresh air
and that's the damn truth

yeh my sis, let me spit this
never give up
here's my hand and my heart
for all the people I love
gotta walk this track
I always got your back
I'll be there whatever weather
you can trust in that

well you can trust that it's difficult
tricky to open up
difficult to trust another
when you're down on your luck
but you can bet
when you talk about your struggle and stress
it's like the weight of the world
is lifted up off your chest

I back my little sis
learn her wrong from right
coz I love ya, Shae
never letting you out of my sight
blackfella never one out
my crew stay tight
coz once you're BT Dub, cuz
you in it for life «

LEAD THE WAY

» THE LIGHTHOUSE MOB

» you wanna be with me?
you wanna be mine?
true love so good
you'd think it's a crime
it's a little early
comin' with those lines
let's wait, take it slow
take time

we don't wanna end up on Dr Phil
boy, take a pill
plus take a chill
kick back, kussa
if you think you're gonna hit that
matha, sit back
relax and rethink that

I'm a boss, gummah
yeah you sabeh me
I take control
you don't control me
those are my rules
I keep it OG
and that's the way
I'm gonna stay, homie

we gonna lead the way
we sick of all of the pain
I can see the change
feel it beat in my veins

LOVE
TRUST
UH-HUH

if we could all see the same
I believe that we could change
we gonna lead the way
we gonna lead the way
we wanna see some change
don't wanna feel the pain
make it a brighter day
coz we're gonna lead the way

respect your lady
never threaten her
respect yourself
coz you are first
show affection
without the hurt
building connection
for better not worst

she's my one an' only
she be my royalty
you my priority
I'll treat you with loyalty
I'm a young man
tryna understand
how I can treat you properly
nothing is stopping me
I'm speaking with honesty
all of my brothers come follow me
this is the way that it's got to be «

BRINGIN' IT BACK

» THE TIN TOWN TRACKERS

» yaama* to my people
mountain to the marshes
come follow us
we be the Boora Mathas
yarn getting started
my family tree
from my Nan and Pop
passed down to me

we be
real deadly like a king brown
kickin' where the creek
meet the river all the way to Tin Town
welcome to Coonamble
I tell ya what
it's a full-time job
representin' my mob

we got
a lotta grog
a lotta sick people
sick of seeing kids
having kids dropping needles
ya brain sizzled up like a barbecue
now I'm stuck in the middle
I know it's hard for you
got kids doing things
that only grown-ups do
doing drugs, shooting up
it ain't nothing new

too shame, too much blame
and not enough game

not a lotta talk
and even less change

ya gotta learn where ya come from first
second: learn your connection to the earth
third: kick ya damn shame to the dirt
ya gotta learn ya culture to know what ya worth

ask the experts
like ya nan and ya pop
be strong
steer clear of the yaandi* and grog
be what?
nup, never be afraid to dream
it's strong, young leaders our people need

it's the Tin Town rappers
we tracking the facts
as a matter of fact
having a crack at bringing culture back
mud map and a mic in my backpack
word like a weapon getting ready to attack

coz I believe in my people
I believe in my health
I respect my ancestors
and respect myself
I believe I will receive
what I need to be me
I believe

I see your strength
I see your pride
I see you been through a hell of a ride
I see that fire burns inside
I see that twinkle in your eye «

** see glossary pp. 165-172 for translations*

REACH OUT

» THE TIN TOWN TRACKERS

» let me tell ya little story 'bout me, 'bout you
'bout who?
'bout one in three people in my crew
that's the truth
where's it comin' from?
Tin Town Trackers back with another song
come along

started off pullin' back
stayin' home
no school
head down
won't answer the phone
always alone
entering the danger zone
dealer or the bottle-o
destination unknown

she started off stressing hard
heart beating fast
all strung out like the strings on a guitar
can't concentrate in class
scared she won't pass
disastrous marks
from honor roll to last

it's a common thing
real talk – true
breaking down real walls
Tin Town treatment for the blue

me and you
fixing ya view

no ya not crazy, ya sick like the flu
and that's the truth

it's okay to say you don't feel okay
no shame
reach out and communicate
Tin Town got ya back all day
I know it's hard but you just gotta say

I caught him down the street after class
worried 'bout my brother
man, thought I'd better ask
talk about the past
maybe have a little laugh
let him know that if he needs a friend
all he need to do is ask

I caught her outside the gate
I wanted to talk but she wouldn't wait
she was in a bad state
blood pumping heart rate
take a deep breath sis
slow down
I can wait
I'm ya mate

it's a common thing from the commoner to the king
won't discriminate based on the color of ya skin
no shame in communicating
break it down
gather round
bring it in
let's begin

in the end it all boils down to me
coz I'm the only one that sees what I see
never feel shame
when ya feel pain
that's just a chemical imbalance in ya brain «

IV | PRIDE IN MY PEOPLE

PRIDELANDS

» OUTLAWZ

» put ya marras up: Murrawarri, Budjidi Nation
Yandabulla, Caywarra, Currawinya Station
forced migration from colonisation
taken from my homeland, the place of my creation

I feel incomplete – feel like I'm at a standstill
half my mob buried at Dead Man's Sandhill
I feel incomplete – my river turned into a creek
my spirit's in a language that I don't know how to speak

my destiny at my feet, where the Warrego flow
where the mud dries up because the river's so low
but we know it fo' sho', Prideland with my brothers
we the Outlawz – hunting every day for wild tucker

we the paddymelon, goanna people that's my Dreaming
feeding on the booglie*, the goolberries, the emus
porcupine, bush turkey, googah*, good eating
hunting any season – yep for any reason

strong and proud people, out here we must be
trust me, cuz, you on outlaw country
summer gets dusty, winter gets cold
sittin' round the fire burning Gidgee coal

more trees, more breeze, more ease, more free
don't need concrete up under my feet
got what I need, that's my family
young people, old people come stand up with me

don't wait, step up now, we the original traditional
spiritual Indigenous people with unconditional love
so check it out what we startin'
waste management and a bush tucker garden

a leader is passionate about freedom – pay attention to
role models
we need 'em, can't beat 'em
so we breed 'em and we teach 'em – that knowledge is
power
like the ancestors taught us until their last hours

so what's stopping ya – what the pressure is on top of ya
Enngonia be looking after country – yeah, that's proper,
brah
warrma*, dropping this modern-day corroboree
when ancestors follow me, my bloodline's quality «

* *see glossary pp. 165-172 for translations*

DREAMS

» B-TOWN WARRIORS

» Ngemba, Kunja, Wonkamurra
one in a mill
Barkanji, Gomeroi, Mutawarri
reppin' Bourke still
blackfellas
we were here before Bourke and Wills
now the B-Town Warriors
are back for the kill

sick of seeing Bourke people
doing it tough
it's like every generation
going through the same stuff
death, drugs, babies and jail
we out on bail
anyone'd thinks the system
wants Bourke to fail

young leaders where you at?
right here, right here
this is fire on the track
yep right in ya ear
get ya chin up, cuz
ya better wipe that tear
it's the BT Dub
we all pride, no fear

brother Kayle got a dream – fancy that
I'm gunna be a bush lawyer, lah – proud and black
don't matter what they say – can't hold us back
at least I'm game enough to give it a crack – ooh snap!

I know I can
I know I am
I know that I will be
dream, I can dream

don't be scared to take a chance
take a risk, make a fist
stand tall, work hard
break the chain, make a wish
write a list, write a track
sound deadly? there it is
like BRRRT there it is
like AHA there it is

sick of small-town talk
people running me down
people trying to ankle tap me
trying to take my crown
love and respect for my people
but I'm standing my ground
I do whatever it takes
to make all of my people proud

too scared to have a go
ya don't ya never know
ya never plant a seed
then ya dreams will never grow
'nother culture, song, story, sis
don't mean nothing
we bleed the same colour blood, bud
who ya bluffin'?

it's hard to dream
when ya livin' in a nightmare
when all they see is negative
and that become repetitive
getting blamed for what we never did
me and my relatives
getting difficult to dream
in this town that I live

I know I can
I know I am
I know my gift
and here it is
it's in my blood
with the BT Dub
make a fist
my blackness ain't the color of my skin
my spirit flow from within «

FLY BACK HOME

» THE DESERT SEVENZ

» in the beginning
let it begin
a Dreamtime story
of the spirit within
stomp on the blood red dirt
Alyawarr – black skin
boomerang clap as the thompwa* sing

it was a different age
back in the past
when the Alyawarr people
walked the spinifex grass
from the start we would dance
to the sound of the song
from the beginning of time
we were happy and strong

whoa!
winnianno*
pitchenammo gwerr*
a ghost or another spirit
from another world
change came quick
for the Alyawarr Nation
all work, no pay
back on the cattle station

** see glossary pp. 165-172 for translations*

my people drinking
my people fighting
my people suicide
my people dying
my people crying
lost and alone
dream like an emu, brother
fly back home
my brother keep dreaming
fly back home
fly back home to me
when you gunna fly back home to me?

I too have a dream
I still got hope
don't drink that coke
and don't light that smoke
brother turn the sound up
culture hold the ground up
listen to the spirit in the wind
singin' around us
go to school
learn my culture
how to sing my song
be a dreamer
a leader
and live life long
sing along
with the people
of the Alyawarr Nations
coz change gunna come
with this generation! «

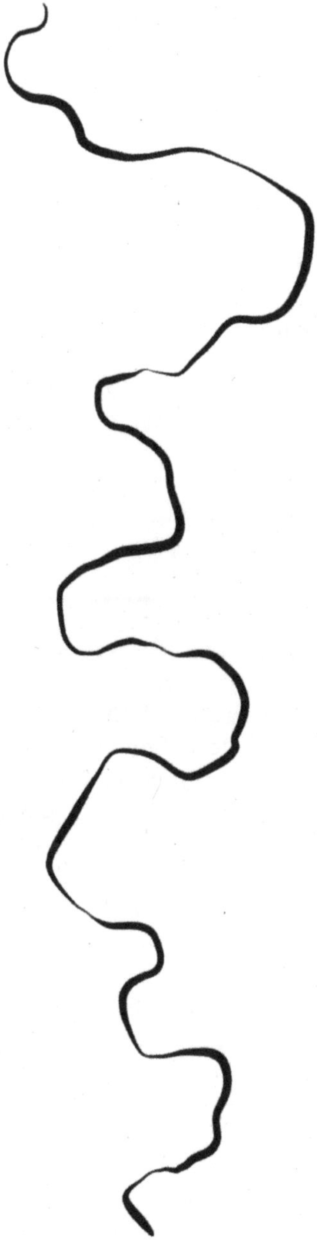

TWO WAYZ

» DESERT SEVENZ

» we were born in the red dirt
raised in Ampilatwatja
comin' with a rap and a spear
we runnin' this
comin' in a 4WD
the Alyawarr tribe
singin' in the moonlight

I was a young brother
doin' my thing
Biggie
Wu-Tang
Tupac the king

nantera Alywarr ngerra	we are all Alyawarr people
nantera kultura dompenamati	learn from the old people
awillichek dompenamati	listen to the old people
dompenamati	old people

I was a bad kid since I was eleven
left school to play 007
no lesson, can't read or write
means life ain't nothin' but a fight
aight?

we the heavyweight crew
be proud of my brother and my cousin and my nephew
yes, you!
S to the T to the R to the ONG
brother born free

young brother, don't make the same mistake
young brother, be strong and pave the way
white fella, atouelpel*
we livin' two ways

sit down with the old people, listen
dance to the Alyawarr rhythm
strong people living
sharing our vision
bounce like a roo
on a brand new mission
on my own two feet
never shame to speak
Desert Sevenz on a red dirt beat

Jessalenco, Tarantino   in the desert we go
Cassius and Meeno   heave ho
Dalton, Shamari, Harrison
Alyawarr   on the land of my great grandfather
Alyawarr Alyawarr   we never too shame to speak
from Alice Springs
we head north-east
to the land of the kangaroo dreaming
hear the wind speaking «

** see glossary pp. 165-172 for translations*

NEW FUTURE, REACHING HIGH

» THE LÚRRA COLLECTIVE

» KK Boys
ready to make noise
binning* bungul* brothers
on the track
this is for my daluk*
and my gogok*
we bringin' that respect back

too much jealousy
too much fighting
too much violence
in Maningrida town
got grog and drugs and sadness
Aruk binning* all stressing out

my Kinship system
my infinite wisdom
Djomi* spring dreamchild
gappa* life-giving
feel my rhythm flow
Djebbana women know
where the wind blow
which way you gonna go?

follow the right road, my daughters
right road
that's what my mumma taught us
stay in the light
respect your sacred site
it's your choice
your basic right

yawadin yawgeow	young boys and young girls
gurrimriy gonda	come here
gunwalk gurribakal	listen to the word
mayála narima	respect and knowledge, keep it
yíberra barra káburla	all the old people
narradjákibba	young women
na' naya néyarra	look out for each other

respect   learn
teach   grow
culture like roots in the land below
strength   support
listen   know
my bloodline strong like the ocean flow

step one:
be education
my people been here
since first creation
next step discipline
dedication
hear it bangin' out
on the radio station

** see glossary pp. 165-172 for translations*

welcome to the future
next level us
in my family
I continue to trust
adjust
imma be a leader
yeah
family
bloodline
beats in my chest

gonna be the best person I can be
Yirritja*
Dhuwa*
my moiety
my family
my family tree
reaching high
and my roots go deep «

** see glossary pp. 165-172 for translations*

CULTURE REMAINZ (I AM THE FUTURE)

» TAGAI BUWAY

» Kaiwalawgal	Inner Islanders
Maluilgal	Near Western Islanders
Guda Maluiglgal	Top Western Islanders
Kulkalgal	Central Islanders
Kemer Kemer Meriam	Eastern Islanders

wiswei* my pamle	how are you my families
where yupla gor?	where are you going?

where the Tagai* shine
and the sager* blow
white sand, blue sea
where the wongai grow
this TI, Tagai* Buway, OH!

north, south, east, west
we representing the Zenadh Kes
Island dress
bu shell* come
Warup
kap kar
pite the thrum!

Kaka nali Kari ker kerem	I am the future
Ngay wagelaw goeygapa	I am the future
Kaka nali Kari ker kerem	I am the future
Ngalpa wagel goeygayka	we are the future

Zuzis to skinnies
canoes to dinghies
Dharis to snap-backs
Maka mak to Air Jordies
turtle to Big Mac
dugong to snack pack
Kapkar, warup, kulap to rap track
dress code, language, diet changed
pride in yumi* culture remains
four winds at my back
my plans are made
warrior blood flowing in my veins
Bipor Taim peeps
got ruled by the man
ration system
no pride, no land
slap to the face
my people of the Straits
never even got a chance
to dice they own place

don't just mark time
it's time to move on
one voice
create a new song
bigger than King Kong
it's island rap
I am the future
best believe that! «

---

* *see glossary pp. 165-172 for translations*

MY CONNECTION

» BOONINGBAH GOORIS

goway goway	come here, come here
woombing goway	welcome, come here
gulga-jaly	collect firewood
weburaar gayeh	make fire

jingi wallah walu-baying ngallinga menji*
that's what my ancestors hand me, my Goodjinburra family
binungu ngalungi, listen and look
a yarn you can't read in a book from way before Captain Cook

this is the place with the smell of salt on the breeze
all of my Gs, Gooris, please, we livin' with ease
catch us surfin' waves with our mates on the beach
we break free like the whales when they breach

garrama*, nymbalin*, respect, contribute — that's my connection
the lore that keep it flowin' in the right direction
keep this love tight, head down the blue-hole for a mud fight
respect and contribute, that's how it's done right

Booningbah, the homeland that we all gotta respect
we the deadly Goodjinburra mob, trying to connect
the key to education is communication
and dedication and don't you ever forget

UNIFIED WE STAND you can never break us down
TOGETHER ON THIS SACRED LAND
check it out – Gudjinburra ground
SOMEWHERE BETWEEN THE SKY, SEA, SAND
look around, look out now!
UNIFIED WE STAND rise up, rise up, rise up

yeah, there's a whole lot of us in this coastal bunch
saltwater mob yeah, ya know what we want
feel our energy rolling in like the swell
positive vibes only, we want you to be well

we wanna show you around, how to connect to the land
everybody's welcome, every woman, child and man
so please don't cross no lines in the sand
respect everything, everywhere that you stand

ya don't know ya story, ya lost
ya don't know ya history, ya wires get crossed
saltwater mob – Booningbar my town
Fingal Head, represent sacred ground

look around — gotta find balance in this life of mine
I gotta find harmony in body and mind
got a fine line between the sky, sea and sand
we gotta come together coz united we stand

** see glossary pp. 165-172 for translations*

YOU + ME

» THE COLLY CREW

» close your eyes and think back
to when the river ran clear
there was love and laughter
we held family dear
with no fear
we reppin' Collarenebri right here
coming back like a boomerang
to sharpen your spear

open your ear, listen up
this a Dreamtime track
from the past to the present
bringing harmony back
yeah, we starting with fact
moving to right now
you're just talking about harmony
we showing you how

all the colours together
we kicking up the red dust
connect
communicate
create a culture of trust
all around the world
living together is a must
because you + me
= us

discrimination
racism and fear
you're not welcome anywhere
and definitely not here
it's prejudice
gammin'* attitudes and hate
it's a little bit of harmony
we trying to create
so get up and set it off
set it up today
Collarenebri Crew
are going to pave the way
respect and understanding
are here to stay
we should celebrate
and live in harmony every day

yep, you + me = us, cuz
they call us the Barwon Boys
respect and understanding is a must, bruz
get up and raise your voice
open your eyes
and think big
coz there's a change in the weather
mobs coming together
open your eyes
and just give
not for worse
but for better
forever and ever
and ever and ever «

FOR MY PEOPLE

» THE COLLI CREW

» well you don't have to be a copper
or black tracker to see that
unstoppable, droppin' on
the top of the drum track
jump like ya sat on a thumbtack
it's the Colli Crew come back
been there, seen and done that

rugrats
wiser and older
night gets colder
boy turn to soldier
life behind the eye
of the beholder
copped the cold shoulder
roll on like a boulder

just like I told ya
break the chain
the Colli Crew back
come change the game
haters gunna hate
jealous gunna blame
attacking from the back
will turn a rapper to a renegade

let 'em say
what they gunna say
Colli Crew any day
is it a bird or is it a plane?
fact is ain't much changed
Colli Crew pump like blood in my veins

gotta stand strong for my people
gunna rap till they make it illegal
gotta say my piece, gotta chase my dream
look, Colli Crew back on the sequel

I'm about five foot two
Gamilaraay boy
black from my cap to my shoe
back rappin' on the mic for you
stat
cuz – how do you do?
flash, fresh
how bout you?
Colli Crew what?
I'm eighteen and my dream
is to spit from the cliff top
Colli hip-hop got it zip-locked
gone through the gift shop
me and my brother
from another mother will lift off

wait
did y'all think I forgot?
I got dissed because I rapped
and tried to be something I'm not
the colour of my skin
is how they used to get their win
they be like "oh he's light
how bout we just pick on him"
let it begin

I'm a fair-skinned brother
yeah, my old man's white
I had a black grandmother
got a handful, a mad crew
of bad black brothers
we stand alone
but got strength in numbers

I been doing it tough
head down, eyes red
by my mother's bed
a Murri understand life and death
because they ain't coming back
once they put to rest
but what's next?

I promised my mum
I'd never stop
so I ain't gunna stop
until I'm sitting at the very top
calling shots
representing my mob
head down
fist up
Gamilaraay
full stop «

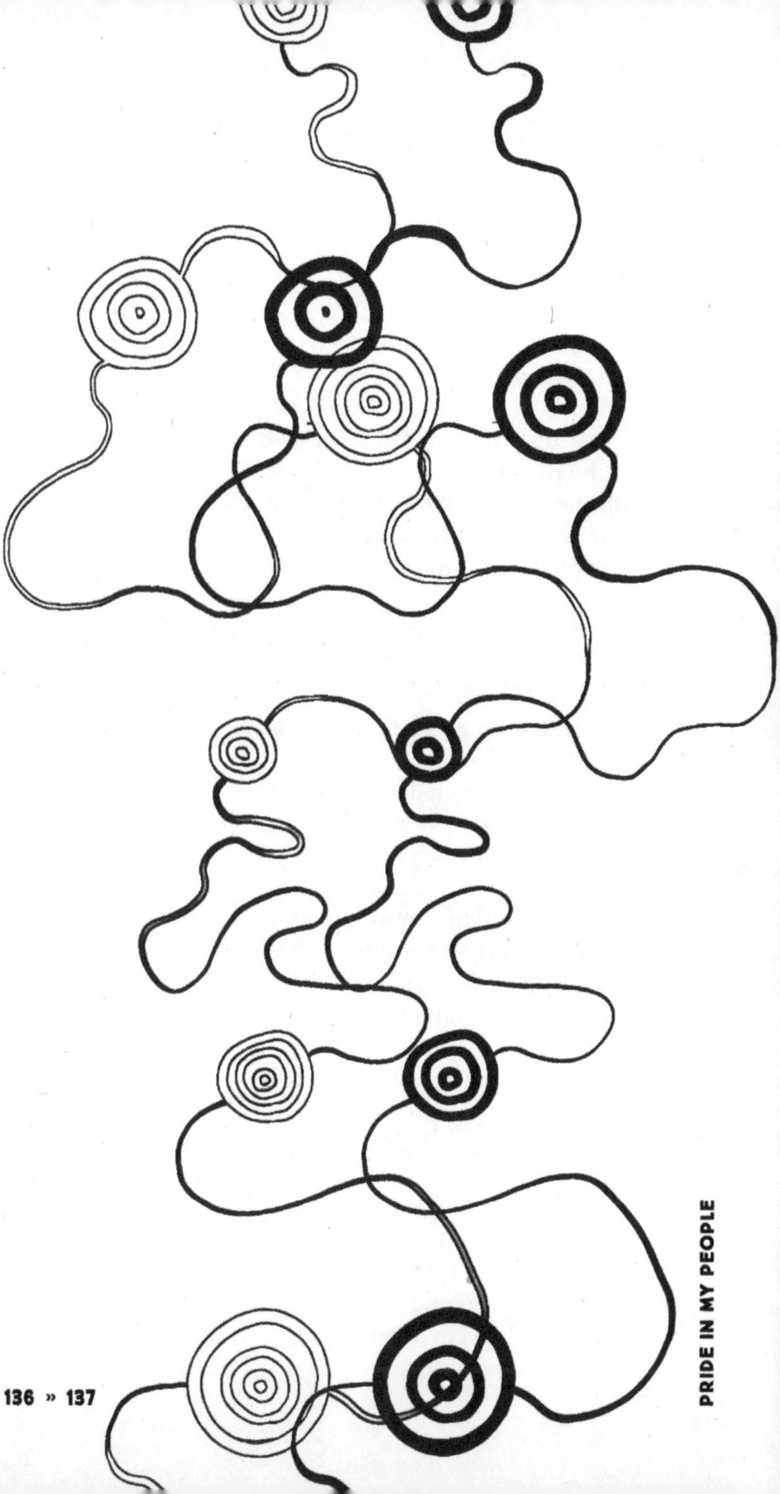

CALLING ME HOME

» GITHABUL: NEXT GENERATION

» eeyah where ya goin?
what's it matter to you?
true!
come up to Bulls and kick back with the crew
nah I'm right
she been acting kinda down and out
she been spinning out just like
she on the Southside Roundabout

I been munchin' out on chips and gravy
on my couch, budda*
KFC and Maccas
I don't wanna get no bush tucker
I feel incomplete
like I'm trippin on defeat
I look into the mirror
and a tear roll down my cheek

this some real life running
man this ain't no Fortnite
bruz, you stayed up all night again
playing games until the sunrise
if you looking for advice
I can show you how it's done right
bush tucker, exercise
soak up in the sunlight

mind, body and spirit
I just can't feel it, can't hear it
even when I'm listening
mind body and soul
wherever I go I'm never alone

buburahnee nuthungully calling me home
making me strong
telling me i'm never alone

buburahnee nuthungully calling me home
making me strong
telling me I'm never alone.

eeyah where ya going?
imma find me some help
I been gone for a minute
I been trying to find myself
I'm strong and I'm with it
I'm going to look after my health
it's the Githabul spirit
it's the feeling that you felt

I been munching out on jalum and boonidj* and binging,
see?
on djuburt, gurruman* whatever my country is giving me
Yumbalay yumbalay move it along I'm proving them
wrong
I reconnect to my country that has kept me strong

I know where I'm going coz I know where I been
I know my spirit's in my bloodline under my skin
my next of kin – stories of the Githabul Nation
passed down from generation to generation let it begin

home is where Djalgumbunj is
spirit and country sing
and my heart is listening «

** see glossary pp. 165-172 for translations*

TWO WORLDS

» *TAGAI BUWAY*

» sound the bu shell*, bala*
yep, my warriors prepare
for a battle of balance
I got a yarn to share
never scared
Igililmay* Ngurpay
flow like my bloodline
Tagai Buway back
and it's crunch time

welcome to the frontline
land of the four winds
life in the sunshine
new day dawning
hit 'em with a punchline
bu shell* calling
hit 'em with a warning
dark cloud forming

habits getting bad
looking for swag
where ya dhari*, bala*?
nah swap him for a doo rag
doin' ya tag
gotta nicko in ya schoolbag
never forget the true colours of ya flag

ya totem and ya clan
come bai gen, young bala*
listen to the wishes of your ama
learn from your aka
ya grandmother
truth, minna pawa*
yumi* inner power
every minute
every hour

in these two worlds we will survive
as sure as the sun will rise
four winds, blue sea and starry sky
following my Tagai*

not from NY
but I rep the eastside
westside of the Torres Strait
where I reside
look to the left, yep
warriors at my side
better steady my weaponry
getting ready to fight

fly like the goeynaw*
we always soaring
gotta learn my culture
through song and story
cut back
just like that
bit of boom bap
culture locked down
like island rap

** see glossary pp. 165-172 for translations*

dressed to impress, yes
all day long
reppin' Zenath Kes – check
we two-way strong
I know where I come from
stand at the border
balancing two ways
with the new world order
it's a tricky track
lookin' back gotta stay true
got an outboard motor
on my dugout canoe
the Tagai* Buway crew
bringin' something brand new
with a can-do kinda attitude

in these two worlds we will survive
as sure as the sun will rise
four winds, blue sea and starry sky
following my Tagai* «

WHO I AM

» THE CONDO CREW FT. ROY PETERSON

» it's true, been here for a long time
my crew got a mad new songline
truth is that back in the day
my culture quickly stripped away

my aunty was a prisoner on her own land
life in a tin shack ruled by the white man
used like an old rag with a dog tag
goin' mad, got banned just for being who I am

gee sad
like ration week
banned from the café
nothing to eat
banned from the cinema
banned from the pool
banned from the bus
gotta walk to school

coz it's a new age in the Bronx
chased by the cops
followed in the shops
yaandi* and grog
when's it gunna stop?
from the bottom
had to battle to the top
power to the black hip-hop
power to the black hip-hop

---

* *see glossary pp. 165-172 for translations*

yalmanbirra
teach
yindyamarra*
respect
winhangarra
learn
walmanbiya
think
listen
hear
learn
respect
respect

been here since the first sunrise
breaming dancing dust at first light
pride in my people
pride in my clan
yamma dumarung*, cuz
sacred land
check it out people
back on the track now
never back down
we adapt to the background
mad black sound
mad black sound «

** see glossary pp. 165-172 for translations*

CREDITS

P2 HEARTBEAT

Wilcannia Barkindji Soldiers » Frances Dutton, Talyssa Dutton, Lamia Jones, Lakaya Dutton, Tia Whyman, Rhianna Harris, Jessii Johnson, Bonni Kinsela, Theresa Bugmy, Bama Johnson, Knomi Johnson, Paul Murray, Jasmine Johnson, Asipeli Williams, Naydine Whyman, Nerida Whyman, Ethan Harris, Toby Finlayson, Jared Melrose

P6 WHERE THE EAGLE ROAMS

Connie Crew » Kayla Hall, Dion Harris, Aurora Gleeson, Daniel Hunt, Brayden Johnson, Alex Mitchell, Jason Mitchell, Karl Carroll, Jaiden Johnson, Briley Etrich, Greg Mckellar, Laurel Andrews Tyler Johnson, Jemma Clifford, Karneisha Taylor, Grace Williams Rigby, Lois Taylor, Linda Hunter, Lindsay Kennedy, Jaharlyn Mitchell, Aunty Mary Mitchell, Toby Finlayson, Josh Nicholas

P8 RIVER TO THE SEA

360 Crew » Destinee Walker, Kaia Louise Mercy, Latifah Taylor, Marlene Rapmund, Jaidia Boney, Brianna Roberts, Georgie Armer, Melanie Laurie, Jaydah Shone, Isabella Mercy-Bushell, Joshua Hippi, Harrison Armer, Brian Quinlin-Randall, Peter Kennedy, Noah Shone, Jake McLeay, Shane Mitchell, Craig Mercy-Bushell and Nicholas Torrens, Toby Finlayson, Josh Nicholas, Jannali Donncaster

P10 BREAKING HABITS

Githabul Next Generation » Toby Finlayson, Michael Graham, Josh Nicholas, Clinton Williams, Jemimah Williams, Gideon Williams, Shemaaya Williams, Maddison Riley, Shonriqua Hippi, Lerqayne Hippi, Shiloh Williams, Athol Hickling, Ashanti Hickling, Justina Williams, Jeremiah Williams, Nathaneal Hickling

P14 OUR COUNTRY, OUR WAY

The Wilcannia Mob: Intergeneration » Toby Finlayson, Michael Graham, Caylam Jones, Jared Melrose, Mason Harris, Gus Kennedy, Rhonda Smith, Elaina Harris, Tia Whyman, Joyce Shepherd, Susan Johnson, Dorothy Mills, Walpra Thompson, Brendan Adams

P18 **DEEP SEA DREAMING**

Bowen Connection » Nevina Noakes Wigg, Cordelia Flack, Djesi Bray, Zion Prior, Lachelle Power, Cygnet Tamwoy, Dudley Dotoi, Ryan Oliver, Samantha Tapin, Linda Illin, Kyiera Nicol, Trinity Ives, Warwick Paul, Declan Marou, Harry Doolan, Bryce Power, Emanuel Parter, Jermellah Toby, Tiana Power, Gareth Prior, Toby Finlayson, Coedie McCarthy

P21 **DHINAWAN TOUCH THE STARS**

The Mob » Toby Finlayson, Michael Graham, Payton Thorne, Markell Trindall, Fred Leone, Lewis Ellis, Malakai Walford, Duncan Murphy

P24 **LOOKING OUT FOR COUNTRY**

Githabul Next Generation » Clinton Williams, Jemimah Williams, Gideon Williams, Jermaine Close, Marshall Close, Malaya Close, Shemaaya Williams, Solomon Williams, Hank Veivers, Alice Close, Amos Close, Memphis Hoskins, Shelby Hoskins, Maddison Riley, Aleisha Riley, Dyllan Fleming, Shonriqua Hippi, Lerqayne Hippi, Shiloh Williams, Renae Williams, Armoni Hickling, Athol Hickling, Ashanti Hickling, Attalia Hickling, Justina Williams, Shynarah Williams, Leroy Brown, Jaylei Brown, Hezekiah Brown, Eerol Brown, Jarius Williams, Jeremiah Williams, Jacob Close, Thane Williams, Declan Furber-Gillick, Toby Finlayson

P26 **PMARA NURNAKA (GOOD COUNTRY)**

Ntaria Connect » Toby Finlayson, Josh Nicholas, Jannali Donncaster, Cassie Williams, Tyrone Malthouse, Guy Sultan, Kiaasha Hall, Shalara Mitchell, Alfie Angus, Shibani Sharpe, Ashanie Raggett, Sheila Armstrong, Lawrence Inkamla, Cliffy Raggett, Jamie Fejo, Matthew Moketaeinja, James Abbott, Owen Jackson, Jonathon Parenoultja, Ricco Swan

P28 **HOMELAND CALLING**

The Lurra Collective » Victor Rostron, Natalie Carey, Toby Finlayson, Joel Westlake, Joseph Diddo, Shayne Nabegeyo, Jack Natilil, Stanley Rankin, Crusoe Kurrdal

P30 **PEOPLE OF THE MOUNTAINS AND THE SEA**

The Black Ducks » Toby Finlayson, Joel Westlake, Ozzie Cruse, Desmond Clapman, Izaiah Aldridge, Jeremiah Bamblett, Liam Hosford, Natalia Croaker, Shane Moore, Tallara Stewart, Tonia Russell

P33 **PUUYA KUNTHA**

Iron Range Danger Gang » Toby Finlayson, Coedie McCarthy, Paddy Hobson, Edwin Pascoe, Ebony Butcher, Shauretta Claudie, Esther Hobson, Ricardo O'Brien, Ross Omenyo, Noongi Taviliniu-Valu Pittard, Kaden Warradoo, Shenika Butcher, Lilita Giblet, Shauna Hobson, Shaznae Kennell, Alinah Macumboy, Erin Accoom, Montaya Bosuen, Fifi O'Brien

P36 **ONE SONGLINE**

The Lúrra Collective » Toby Finlayson, Joel Westlake, Natalie Carey, Tainui Little, Shakira Darcy, Shianne Namarrchi Davis, Zenayha Doolan, Debbie James, Caroline Garwulga, Joseph Diddo, Hamish Garwulgu, Solomon Garwulgu, Cameron Garwulgu, Debbie James, Jonah Ryan, Zephriah Taylor, Adrien Bonson

P38 **WHERE I'M FROM**

Boomalli » Michael Graham

P44 **WHAT WE CAN DO**

Cowra Crew » Lavinus Howarth, Kira Williams, Tsharnah Murray, Jayden Williams, Alyssa Murray, Kyle Morgan, Zipporah Austin, Ezekiel Austin, Matthew Bell, Curtis Bell, Stassi Austin, Elijah Austin, Ethan Austin, Lily Wright, Ashleigh Doolan, Kristy Bell, Le'Shere Williams Doolan, Michael Howarth, Treydon Howarth, Lusi Austin, Toby Finlayson

P48 **TIME WILL TELL**

Bwgcolman Mob » Ricky Johnson, Nashae Bulsey, Martin Kennedy, Elizabeth Doomadgee, Jahlen Doomadgee, Sian Daisy, Kevin Inkerman, Shameka Sam, Sharona Sam, Frederick Ketchup, Bernard Blanket, Ekunya Reuben, Lex Fulford, Tianiwa Bulsey, Toby Finlayson, Ciolla Riley

P50 **THE REAL WORLD**

Culture Connect » Cassey Dukes, Jerri Tomkinson, Mark Cobb, Emily Molloy, Ben Molloy, Bridie Hughes, Hannah Thorpe, Tamika Cohen, Jye Sloane, Jaylin Wave, Matty Duke, Macca Dalton, Latarsha Johnson, Whitney Duffy, Jai Nolan, Billie-Jo Crisp, Lily Walsh, Kaidyn Haynes Le'Kiesha-Lee Bodwen, Marley Carr, Kirra Nean, Kay Mulligan, Barry Merritt, Toby Finlayson, Josh Nicholas

P52 **STATE OF THE HEART**

Deni Mob » Karen Wilson, Tyron Ross Garden, Malaki Lake, Naoka Owen, Lee Walton, Arizona Buckley, Destiny Neilson, April Weir, Benicio Glass, Chloe Hammond, Billi Jo Austin, Cyrus Buckley, Sam Carter, Shelby Owen, Shyanne Smith, Lacrisia Biles Dixon, KEyontai Biles Dixon, Amanda Laxon, Rani Briggs, Declan Furber-Gillick, Toby Finlayson

P56 **WHERE YA FROM?**

BoggaMish » Maleisha Woodbridge, Sienna Craigie, Nahum McGrady, Keleisha Duncan, Benji Boland, Fred Gillian, Matayla Boland, Brodie Armstrong, Emma Hinch, Tamarah McGrady, Cherise Hinch, Kianna Troutman, Amarli McGrady, Shakeilah Dennison, Daneisha Williams, Fran McGrady, Elaine Edwards, Shanelle Hippi, Dustin Close, Toby Finlayson

P58 **ABORIGINAL JUSTICE**

The PI Boys » Morris Walsh, Patrick Seaton, Matthew Priestley, Kiefer Walsh, Toby Finlayson

P62 **SMALL ISLAND, BIG FIGHT**

Irwarpaup ft. Tamyok » Toby Finlayson, Gail Mabo, Frank Nagai, Joel Westlake, Tristen Passi, Azaliah Salee, Swana Salee, Ray Noah, Cathy Marou, Lillah Passi, Raffi Wailu, Anai Ghee, Marcus Kudib, Tagai Tapau-Bon, Teonii Atkin, Norm Marou, Taiku Wailu, Tomasina Bon, Gagee Barsa, McFarlane Noah, Way Day, Edward Noah, April Tabo, Cabaan Salee

P64 **THE WILD MID-WEST**

Mully Mob » Bobbie Merry, Wayleen Merry, Dean Oliver, Ted Harvey, Georgina Papertalk, Quentin Simpson, Shauntae Derschow, Dominic Whitby, Whitney Comeagain, Glenda Comeagain, Jaekyah Derschow, Channy Mitchell, Shakira Collins, Dennis Simpson, Amber Little, Patrick Ryder, Lex Harvey, Skyla Jackamarra, Rosemary Merrit, Aaeliaha Merrit, Kiaha Gelby, Zetalia Gelby, Toby Finlayson, Joel Westlake

P66 **BUILT TO LAST**

Cairns Murri Crew » Toby Finlayson, Joel Westlake, Denzel Kennedy, Yirgjhilya Laurie

P68 **MY GENERATION**

B-Town Warriors » Jemmah Knight, Lashaye Dutton, Lekeisha Orcher, Lorraine Dutton, Katie Brookson, Nikyra Suckling, Shakayla Dennis, Jedda Smith, Chequita Knight, Robert Kelly, Danika Nean, Jessica Moore, Es Edwards, Elle Edwards, Myah-Rose Edwards-Driscoll, Rozaria Suckling, Tracey Edwards, Laurinia McKellar, Ben Hawdon, Ian Geyer, Amelia Suckling, Deslen Dennis, Sahara Dennis, Leah Dennis, Mahayleigher Dennis, Clancy McKellar, Kayle McKellar, Tallis Orcher, Jorden Dennis, Tyrall Edwards, Kylan Orcher, Toby Finlayson

P71 **TIME WAIT FOR NO-ONE**

Ilan Stylez » Ned David, Talulah Amber, Mawai Whap, Wasada Bani, Katie Pilot, Trudy Mareko, Gagee Barsa, Nataliah Mosby, Andrew Lui, Luke Mosby, Ellen Ronson

P73 **YAEGL BIIRRINBA**

380 Crew » Latifah Taylor, Latoiah Anderson, Charlize Yuke, Isabella Mercy-Bushell, Dawson Vesper, Jaida Boney, Toby Burnes, Taurus Shone, Brianna Roberts, Reece Warburton, Jaydah Shone, Kai Thomsen, Leroy Laurie, Melanie Laurie, Rebecca Shannon, Destinee Walker, Billy Woods, Ngheri Kapeen, Nick Torrens, Lilli Kennedy, Zhanae Whalley, Charlotte Williams, Jannali Doncaster, Toby Finlayson

P76 DJABUGANYDJI BAMA

KDA Crew » Ciolla Riley, Max Alpin, Winston Alpin, Dahskeikky Brim, Rosetta Bulow, Charlie Collins, Drayden Lawson, Nolan Lawson, Chloe Richards, Shakactey Riley, Shyriah Williams, Shemaiah Kendrick, Haily Dorante, Amanda Crosbie, Sheree Donahue, Porta James, Santiago Graham, Caesar Hunter, Delta Wason, Toby Finlayson, Coedie McCarthy

P80 CALLING INTO THE DEEP

380 Crew » Zoe Gardiner, Zayke Swan Pearce, William Walker, Tyrelle Waters, Tye Eamens Gardiner, Tyrelle Waters, Walter Donnelly, Toby Burnes, Taurus Shone, Tashiah Woodley, Talia Rooks, Taineisha Byers, Sue Bradley, Uncle Ron Heron, Noah Shone, Melanie Laurie, Ngheri Kapeen, Nicholas Torrens, Lenore Parker, Madison Howarth, Latifah Taylor, Latoiah Anderson, Krystal Randall, Jericho Close, Justin Tapper, Kaia Mercy, Jarrad Williams, Jake Mcleay, Jaida Boney, Hank Williams, Harrison Armer, Isabella Mercy-Bushell, Gloria A. Mercy, Glenda Macphail, Georgie Armer, Elhi Laurie, Callan Obst, Craig Mercy-Bushell, Danny Young, Brianna Roberts, Brian Quinlin-Randall

P84 BRING IT BACK

2820 Crew » Aaron Horan, Allan Riley, Cecil Stanley, Corey Mills, Courtney Cummings, Ellie-May Stanley, Jack Williams, Keely Williams, Kira Meizer Riley, Liam Hilet, Marissa Stanley, Mason Humphries, Mason Peckham, Millie Mills, Nicholas Musgrave, Paige Hillard, Peter Sarsfield, Rhys Meyers, Summah Meizer Riley, Taylor Cummings, Tyreek Frail, Toby Finlayson

P88 SPEAK WITH ME

The Mob » Tyrese Suey, Duncan Murphy, Quincy Dennis, Nyokia Townsend, Serena Sharpley, Janet Murphy, Liam French, Leslie Wallace, Cody Taylor, Chris Murray, Jordan Murray, Zoe Provest, Lewis Ellis, Paul Haley, Latia & Mereki Sabs-Dennis, Abbey & Dainah Ashby, Jaylin & Makayla Duffy, Payten Thorne, Ian & Azaria Dennis, Issac Kennedy, Toby Finlayson

P91 HOW YA FEELIN'

The Condo Crew » Kurrin Brandy, Douglas Smith, Chontelle Dargin, Leah Dargin, Caleb Powell, Ernie Peterson, Tywayne Coe, Douglas Smith, Malcolm Davies, Errol Packham, Joseph Packham, Esther Weatherall, Hope Milson, Anna-Rose Smith, Taya Coe, Tiffiney Dodds, Hayley Richards, Tamera Kirby, Jamall Dargin, Kimhilda Dargin, Walter Smith, Jay Flick, Kaiden Atkinson, Clifton Cubby, Emanuel Peterson, Levi Peterson, Roy Peterson, Nickolle Kirby, Rashard Kirby, Lorenz Pritchard, Toby Finlayson

P93 CHANGES

Wambool Worldwide » Tyson Keogh, Marissa Morgan, Bailey Honeyman, Kyle Tangye, Elizabeth Crean, Charmaine Doolan, Bevan Sampson, Jordan Williams, Nerida Lord, Dulcie Lord, Duaine Wallace, Jake Callaghan, Tyleeah Carberry, Elizabeth Doolan, Bethany Donaldson, Tatiana Bosma, Jade Neilan, Duncan Murphy, Jayden Thornbury, Shanese Lane-Bergan, Toby Finlayson

P96 PEOPLE OF THE RED SUNSET

B-Town Warriors » Toby Finlayson, Michael Graham, Carlo Santone, Don Finlayson, Julie Knight, Sari Wills, Lorraine Dutton, Shavinah Mann, Lekeisha Orcher, Kayle McKellar

P100 THUNDERCLOUD

B Town Warriors » Lekeisha Orcher, Nikyra Suckling, Braith Kelly, Kayle McKellar, Sari Wills, Shakyla Dennis, Jemmah Knight, Shavinah Mann, Katie Brookson, Trey Cahill, Janaya Knight, Jeddah Smith, Rozaria Suckling, Fred Monaghan, Lahshaye Dutton, Ewan Elwood, Ben Hawdon

P103 REWRITE YOUR STORY

B-Town Warriors » Toby Finlayson, Carlo Santone, Janaya Knight, Lekeisha Orcher, Nikyra Suckling, Katie Brookson, Lorraine Dutton

P106 LEAD THE WAY

The Lighthouse Mob » Declan Furber-Gillick, Jannali Donncaster, Holly Robinson, Josh Nicholas, Lokz Saltner, Fred Sibley, Ernest Tapau, Nikayla Tapau, Tianee Tapau, Ngawai Tiera, Lina Tiera, Merlin Massey, Sheldon Hero, Raynard Conway

P108 BRINGIN' IT BACK

The Tin Town Trackers » Joel Westlake, Toby Finlayson, Lydia Smith, Tobiana Glasson, Angie O'Connor, Johnathan Blattman, Ivan Adams, Jayma Cleary, Nadia Boney, Jacob Darcy, Josh Horan, Jarrod Drummond, Damian Davis, Kylah Astill, Killara Darcy, Teresa Smith, Shanaya Kennedy, Taylee Millgate

P110 REACH OUT

The Tin Town Trackers » Toby Finlayson, Joel Westlake, Roy Weiland, Blade Arrowsmith, Samuel Carey, Peppah McMullen, Joshua Streeting, Brody Jordan, Tiffany Hardwick, Mitch Nalder, Kiarna Smith, Brooke Elsley, Kenja Maber, Cheyenne Harvey, Damien Manson, Lyall Dodd, Riley Fernando

P114 **PRIDELANDS**

Outlawz » Ethan Eulo, Gabe Smith, Garren Smith, Germaine Edwards, Jacqueline Campbell, Jahleon Smith, Jahqualyn Kelly, Katrell Monaghan, Raymond Barker, Samuel Shillingsworth, Tannia Edwards, Wayne Kelly, Wesley Kelly, Natarlia Smith, Declan Furber Gillick, Coedie McCarthy, Toby Finlayson

P116 **DREAMS**

B-Town Warriors » Lekeisha Orcher, Nikyra Suckling, Braith Kelly, Kayle McKellar, Jemmah Knight, Shakyla Dennis, Katie Brookson, Trey Cahill, Janaya Knight, Jeddah Smith, Rozaria Suckling, Fred Monaghan, Lahshaye Dutton, Ewan Elwood, Ben Hawdon

P119 **FLY BACK HOME**

The Desert Sevenz » Denzel Elkedra, Shamari Turner, Harrison Morton, Meshak Holmes, Donald Thompson, Preston Payne, Frankie Holmes, Casey Holmes, Sam Petersen, Leon Teece, Farren Bailey, Cassius Morton, Tarantino Morton, Michael Price

P122 **TWO WAYZ**

Desert Sevenz » Denzel Elkedra, Shamari Turner, Harrison Morton, Meshak Holmes, Donald Thompson, Preston Payne, Frankie Holmes, Casey Holmes, Sam Petersen, Leon Teece, Farren Bailey, Cassius Morton, Tarantino Morton, Michael Price

P124 **NEW FUTURE, REACHING HIGH**

The Lúrra Collective » Victor Rostron, Ernest Rostron, Milena Mace, Simika Rostron, Bessalina Wood, Graham Rostron, Johnson Rostron, James Kelly, Alice Eather, Noni Eather, Helen Williams, Cyrus Rostron, Braiden Miller, Toby Finlayson, Natalie Carey, Joel Westlake, Ashlyn Murrimal

P128 **CULTURE REMAINZ (I AM THE FUTURE)**

Tagai Buway » Toby Finlayson, Joel Westlake, Katura Samson-Bob, Pele Savage, Andrew Lui, Noel Repu, Wilfred Mene, Letrell Uta, Yana Tabuai, Madeina David, Samowa Baragud, Tyra Ware, Onice Matthew, Evie Savage

P130 **MY CONNECTION**

Booningbah Gooris » Toby Finlayson, Anthony Martino, Coedie McCarthy, Lyric Tuala, Birren Slabb, Mibin Slabb, Kyle Slabb, Joshua Slabb, Marni Tuala, Jarulah Slab, Raven Tuala, Falon Tuala, Fred Gibson, Dakina Penola, David Gibson, Colin Gibson, Hunter Dee Overall, Jason Tuku-Togo, Kaleb Slabb

SOME NOTES FROM THE EDITOR

WHAT DO WE CALL YOU? WHAT DO YOU CALL YOURSELVES?

As this book demonstrates, there is no 'one' Aboriginal and Torres Strait Islander person. We may have some similarities, but the truth is we are a very diverse people. So, to know what we like to be called, just ask us!

Since invasion, we have been relentlessly defined by others – we prefer to identity ourselves! You'll notice a variety of different ways we express our identity.

The Aboriginal-owned newspaper *Koori Mail* recommends the following hierarchy in order of preference.

- The person's language group, e.g. Wiradjuri.
- The area the person comes from, e.g. Murri (Queensland), Koori/Goori (New South Wales, Victoria), Nunga (South Australia), Noongar (south-west Western Australia), Yolŋu (Arnhem land), Palawa (Tasmania).
- Aboriginal, if from mainland Australia; Torres Strait Islander, if from Queensland's Torres Strait Islands.
- Aboriginal and Torres Strait Islander to be generic.

According to the *Aboriginal and Torres Strait Islander adolescent and youth health and wellbeing 2018* report, a total of 61% of Aboriginal and Torres Strait Islander people aged 10–24 years recognise their traditional homelands or traditional country, and 69% had been involved in cultural events in the previous twelve months.

WHAT IS THE HISTORY AND IMPACT OF GOVERNMENT POLICIES ON ABORIGINAL AND TORRES STRAIT ISLANDER PEOPLE (SINCE 1788)?

We've lived here for tens of thousands of years; the vast majority of human history in Australia is that of Aboriginal and Torres Strait Islander people.

From 1788, Indigenous land was invaded by British colonists on the premise that the land belonged to no-one ('terra nullius'). Frontier violence caused a drastic decline in the Aboriginal and Torres Strait Islander population.

At the University of Newcastle, a group of researchers led by Professor Lyndall Ryan have created "Colonial Frontier Massacres in Australia, 1788-1930", an interactive map that details a timeline of what's been researched about frontier violence. The researchers state:

> *'From the moment the British invaded Australia in 1788 they encountered active resistance from the Aboriginal and Torres Strait Islander owners and custodians of the lands. In the frontier wars which continued until the 1960s massacres became a defining strategy to eradicate that resistance. As a result thousands of Aboriginal men, women and children were killed.'*

As well as random killings and organised massacres, many Indigenous men, women and children died of exposure to introduced diseases such as smallpox, influenza and measles, for which Indigenous communities had no resistance.

Most of those who survived the frontier conflict were forcibly removed from their land and sent to missions or reserves, which had been established in co-operation with the government. For the most part, missions were notoriously brutal places where people were punished for practising their culture or speaking their language. From the end of the nineteenth century, under state and territory laws, protectors, protection boards and native affairs departments segregated and controlled a large part of the Indigenous population. It has been estimated that the Aboriginal and Torres Strait Islander population during the 1920s had fallen to only about 60,000 from perhaps one million people in 1788.

In 1937, the Commonwealth Government held a national conference which agreed that Aboriginal people 'not of full blood' should be absorbed or 'assimilated' into the wider population. This was the beginning of what is known as the protection and assimilation era.

Legislation such as the *Aboriginals Preservation and Protection Act 1939* (Queensland) restricted the lives of Aboriginal and Torres Strait Islanders.

The 1939 law explicitly:

- excluded Aboriginal and Torres Strait Islander peoples from voting in state elections;
- made it unlawful for any Aboriginal or Torres Strait Islander person in Queensland to knowingly receive or possess alcohol;
- restricted movement;
- denied any right to Aboriginal people's lands of their birth or reserve lands; and
- curtailed access to the normal processes of justice available to the rest of the community.

The 1939 law also continued to give the relevant authorities power to:

- resettle by force;
- remove children without proof of neglect;
- forbid marriage without approval;
- censor mail;
- compel reserve residents to work for low wages (or no wages); and
- seize property without consent.

A key part of the assimilation policy that left a devastating legacy was the ongoing forcible removal of Aboriginal and Torres Strait Islander children from their families and their placement into white institutions or foster homes.

The Stolen Generations refers to Indigenous children who, under various Australian federal and state government policies, were forcibly removed from their families. These policies were implemented between approximately 1905 and 1967 but continued illegally into the 1970s.

These victims were denied their family, culture and past, and the cruel implications of these policies have been felt for generations. On 13 February 2008, then prime minister Kevin Rudd issued a formal apology to the Stolen Generations. It was a national acknowledgement of the wrong and harm done by previous governments to Indigenous peoples on the grounds of race-hate and he stated explicitly that this should never occur again. National Sorry Day is observed every year on 26 May. Recent Sorry Days call our attention to the continuing high rates of removal of Aboriginal and Torres Strait Islander children from their families today, with our children ten times more likely to be in the child protection system compared with non-Indigenous children.

Since 1788, our people have been robbed of their freedoms and institutionalisation has been a dominant theme in our lives. Our life choices were dictated much more by government than was the case for non-Aboriginal people, and limitations have been put upon our modes of living, work, financial and leisure activities.

WHAT WAS THE FREEDOM RIDE?

In 1965, a group of University of Sydney students, led by Arrernte and Kalkadoon man Charles Perkins and inspired by the United States 1961 Freedom Rides, got on a bus and toured through New South Wales regional towns such as Walgett, Kempsey, Bowraville and Moree to show wider Australia the experience of Aboriginal Australians. This was a key event in the lead-up to the successful 1967 referendum; thousands of Australians and Aboriginal and Torres Strait Islander peoples campaigned for many decades to achieve the result.

WHAT DID THE 1967 REFERENDUM DO?

Before the 1967 referendum, each state and territory had its own laws in place referring to Aboriginal and Torres Strait Islander people. Many of these state-based laws restricted the lives of Aboriginal and Torres Strait Islanders.

The 1967 referendum proposed two key changes to the Australian constitution:

- to include Aboriginal and Torres Strait Islander people in the census; and
- to allow the federal government to make laws for Aboriginal and Torres Strait Islander people.

An overwhelming amount – 90.77% – of Australians voted YES.

Oodgeroo Noonuccal (Kath Walker), 1967 Referendum Campaign National Coordinator, said that: 'The victory of the 1967 referendum was not a change of white attitudes. The real victory was the spirit of hope and optimism which affected blacks all over Australia. We had won something ... we were visible, hopeful and vocal.'

More than fifty years later, the 1967 referendum remains a significant symbolic moment, but fell short of expectations of lasting change for Aboriginal and Torres Strait Islanders. Many of us are still demanding reforms that will give us a voice in the political institutions established in the constitution.

WHAT IS 'COUNTRY' AND WHAT DOES IT MEAN TO ABORIGINAL AND TORRES STRAIT ISLANDER PEOPLE?

Country is all encompassing – it means more than just land. Country means sky, water, ground, underground and all living things. We say country doesn't belong to us – we belong to country. Our practices and beliefs clash with the European model of land ownership. We believe in sustaining our country as a way of sustaining ourselves.

As part of discussions on climate change, in 2008 the United Nations Permanent Forum on Indigenous Issues raised concerns about the huge challenges Indigenous peoples are facing:

> *'Indigenous people have the smallest ecological footprints in the world's communities and should not be asked to carry the heaviest burden of adjusting to climate change.'*

My essay, 'The Country is like a body', highlights the importance of Indigenous knowledge in climate change response. In this essay I wrote:

> *'Climate change challenges Indigenous identities. Recognising the need for action to safeguard these identities is only the beginning. Indigenous culture needs to do more than just motivate a response to climate change; it needs to be a part of any response. Innovation and resilience have buoyed efforts in the past. They are needed now. If Australia does respond to climate change but does so without seeking the input of its Indigenous people, this response will be perpetuating this country's colonial history.'*

WHAT WAS THE MABO JUDGEMENT?

Eddie 'Koiki' Mabo, a Meriam man from the island of Mer (Murray Island) in the Torres Strait, was a key plaintiff in a landmark land rights case in the High Court of Australia, today referred to as the 'Mabo Case'. The High Court decision in the 'Mabo Case' altered the foundation of land law in Australia. In the following year, the *Native Title Act 1993* was passed through the Australian Parliament and opened the way for further claims of traditional rights to land and compensation.

WHAT ARE TOTEMS?

We use this term to refer to those revered spiritual ancestors that manifest themselves in non-human forms.

WHAT ARE ANCESTORS?

For us, ancestors can refer to the ancestral beings who created every aspect of the landscape and the laws by which people still live. And it can also refer to any deceased person from which an individual or group is descended.

WHAT IS A SONGLINE?

A route through the landscape which is believed to have been travelled during the Dreamtime, and which features a series of landmarks thought to relate to events that happened during this time. A song intended to convey a sacred narrative.

this a call out
from the north to west
and if you know the emu dreaming yarn
y'all connected

'DHINAWAN TOUCH THE STARS' by The Mob

The song title refers to an ancient Kamileroi constellation etched into the negative space of the Milky Way. A powerful and sacred Indigenous songline, the Dhinawan (Emu) story shifts and changes as it travels from nation to nation.

wiimpitcha murndy
seven stars in the night

'HEARTBEAT' by Wilcannia Barkindji Soldiers

The Star Dreaming story of the Seven Sisters is one of the most widely distributed stories throughout Aboriginal Australia. The songline for this story covers more than half the width of the continent, from deep in the Central Desert out to the west coast. This songline travels through many different language groups, and different sections of the narrative are recognised in different parts of the country.

WHAT IS LORE?

The term 'lore' encompasses the religious, spiritual and practical laws that Aboriginal and Torres Strait Islander people observe in their own cultures.

WHAT IS KINSHIP?

Kinship is a complex social system that determines how people relate to each other, and determines their roles, responsibilities and obligations in relation to one another and country. This feature of social organisation and family relationships exists in various forms across Australia.

WHAT ARE SOME CURRENT ISSUES AFFECTING YOUNG ABORIGINAL AND TORRES STRAIT ISLANDER PEOPLE IN AUSTRALIA?

The Aboriginal and Torres Strait Islander population is young. In the 2016 census, the median age was 23 years, compared with 38 years for non-Indigenous Australians; 65% of the Aboriginal and Torres Strait Islander community was less than 30 years old, compared with 39% of non-Indigenous Australians.

A total of 241,824 Indigenous people aged 10–24 years lived in Australia in 2016, representing 5% of the total Australian youth population.

Due to past genocidal policies and continuing effects that make Indigenous people more disadvantaged than other Australians in terms of income, services, housing, employment and education, a lot of our young people are struggling. Young Aboriginal and Torres Strait Islander people may face additional obstacles in making a successful transition to adulthood. The effect of inter-generational trauma, racism and prejudice, and socioeconomic disadvantage are all relevant in understanding the experiences of young Indigenous people today. The general Australian population discriminated against Aboriginal people in many ways, which affected their education, housing, employment, income and self-esteem.

According to the *Aboriginal and Torres Strait Islander adolescent and youth health and wellbeing 2018* report, 67% of Indigenous people aged 15–24 years experienced low to moderate levels of psychological distress.

According to ABS statistics, Aboriginal and Torres Strait Islanders aged between 15 and 24 years are almost four times more likely to commit suicide than non-Indigenous people the same age, and 95% of Aboriginal and Torres Strait Islander people in Australia are affected by a suicide.

Young Indigenous people continue to be over-represented in the justice system, making up 43% of young people under youth-justice supervision in 2014–15. Young Indigenous people are seventeen times more likely to be in detention than other Australians.

One of the key findings of the 1991 Royal Commission into Aboriginal Deaths in Custody was that, 'The causes of over-representation of Aboriginal people in custody are those factors which bring Aboriginal people into conflict with the criminal justice system in the first place ... [and] the most significant contributing factor is the disadvantaged and unequal position in which Aboriginal people find themselves in society.'

WHAT ARE YOU HOPEFUL FOR?

The mob of voices throughout this book often points to hope. How, you may ask, can we have hope under such circumstances? We give each other love and purpose.

Professor Marcia Langton in her book *Welcome to Country* says we are the 'most culturally productive people in the country'. We are in many different artistic and performance roles. Singing, dancing, composing and making music are at the core of Aboriginal and Torres Strait Islander cultures. Artists perform in many different styles – traditional styles as well as contemporary ones; many performers combine the two. They convey connections to culture and country.

Political and powerful, Aboriginal and Torres Strait Islander hip-hop is in an exciting and thriving place, with artists such as Baker Boy, Briggs, Birdz and Kaylah Truth finding a receptive and broad audience.

We are witnessing momentum that gives many of us hope for the future.

The true history of this country, which includes Aboriginal and Torres Strait Islander histories and cultures, is beginning to be taught in schools. Our people have instilled in us resistance and intelligence, and as the Iron Range Danger Gang say, 'puuya kuntha' (strong heart). Lasting change is being created with this generation.

Ellen van Neerven

GLOSSARY

Many young Aboriginal and Torres Strait Islanders are passionate about their languages.

More than 600 distinct language dialects and at least 250 languages were spoken across the continent before colonisation. Australia rapidly changed from being one of the most linguistically diverse places on earth to an illegal occupation determined to extinguish First Nations cultural and language practices. Many governments and organisations, including churches that ran the missions, banned or discouraged Indigenous people from speaking their languages. The term 'linguicide' was coined in 2013 by Professor Ghil'ad Zuckermann, the Chair of Endangered Languages at the University of Adelaide, to describe the loss of languages.

It is remarkable that more than 120 Indigenous languages are still spoken and maintained, and 50 are classed as 'thriving.' The remaining languages are considered 'sleeping'. There are language teaching and revival programs set up right across the country to ensure language will be an inherent right for our young people.

A tool often used in teaching about Aboriginal and Torres Strait Islander languages is the AIATSIS map of Indigenous Australia, available on the AIATSIS website (www.aiatsis.gov.au).

'Aboriginal English' is a dialect of Australian English spoken by most Aboriginal Australians. It is made up of a number of varieties which developed differently in different parts of Australia. These varieties are generally said to fit along a continuum, ranging from forms close to Standard Australian English, to forms closer to Kriol. There are distinctive features of accent, grammar, words and meanings, as well as language use.

'Torres Strait Creole' is a mix of Standard Australian English and traditional languages spoken by most Torres Strait Islanders.

ATHABAD: water

ATOUELPEL (ALYAWARR): blackfella

BAAKA (BARKANJI/PARKANDJI): The name of the Darling River. The Baaka River is at the heart of the Barkindji/Parkandji name and culture.

BAGAAY-GU (GAMILIROI): river

BALA (TORRES STRAIT CREOLE): brother

BALLINDA (YOLŊU MATHA): whitefella

BAMA NGUNGI: mob

BARJI (GAMILARAAY): mother's mother

BAWAA (GAMILARAAY): sister

BIIRRINBA (YAYGIRR): river

BILYARA (PAAKANTJI/BAAKANTJI): eagle

BINNING (YOLŊU MATHA): men

BOOGLIE (MURRAWARRI): yabby

BOONDI (WIRADJURI): hitting stick

BOONIDJ: echidna

BRE (ABBREVIATION): Brewarrina

BRED (SLANG): brother

BU SHELL (TORRES STRAIT): The bu or trumpet shell is blown like a trumpet to summon the clans together or warn of impending danger. It is also used today to summon worshippers to certain church services.

BUDAJJII (DJABUGAY): carpet snake

BUDDA (ABORIGINAL ENGLISH): brother

BULLURRU (DJABUGAY): Creator Spirit

BULLYMAN (ABORIGINAL ENGLISH): police officer

BUNDARRA (DJABUGAY): cassowary

BUNGUL (YOLŊU MATHA): dance/song

BUNJI (DJABUGAY): brother-in-law

BUNNA (YUIN): rain

DALUK (YOLŊU MATHA): women

DARTHAR (GAMILARAAY): mother's father

DHAGAAN (GAMILARAAY): brother

DHAWAAN (GAMILARAAY)/DURAAGAN (YAYGIRR): country

DHARI (TORRES STRAIT CREOLE): is the distinctive traditional dance and ceremonial headdress of the Torres Strait

DHINAWAN (GAMILARAAY): emu ancestor

DHUWA (YOLŊU MATHA): All Yolngu people in north-eastern Arnhem Land belong to one of two basic divisions, or moieties, called Dhuwa and Yirritja

DJAMA (DJABUGAY): snake

DJIDGA (DJABUGAY): sister

DJOMI (YOLŊU MATHA): is seen as a metaphor for the cultural network that exists around the Maningrida area

DULBIL (DJABUGAY): wallaby

DYINDA (YAYGIRR): sister

ESO (TORRES STRAIT CREOLE): thank you

GAGU (YAYGIRR): brother

GAMMIN' (ABORIGINAL ENGLISH): joking

GANGLA (DJABUGAY): kangaroo

GAPPA: water

GARRAMA: respect

GINAGAAY (YAYGIRR): welcome

GOEYNAW: eagle

GOGOK (YOLŊU MATHA): men

GOOGAH (MURRAWARRI): goanna

GUBBA (ABORIGINAL ENGLISH): white person

GUDU: sea/ocean

GUDYUGA (YUIN): young people

GUNYARRA (DJABUGAY): crocodile

GURI BUGA DJUNAL (DJABUGAY): good morning

GURRUGAMA (YUIN): cold westerly wind

GURRUMAN: kangaroo

GWAANI (WIRADJURI): crazy

IGILILMAY NGURPAY (TORRES STRAIT): Top Western Islands

INA NOOMUNLAG: land

IWAYII: crocodile (totem)

JARJUMS (ABORIGINAL ENGLISH): children

JINGI WALLAH WALU-BAYING NGALLINGA MENJI (BUNDJALUNG): hello, how are you?

KAAKA (ARRARNTA): older brother

KAANJU: Indigenous clan name

KES DIEW GASSOMAN: everybody proud

KIIRA KIIRINANHA (BARKINJI/PARKINDKI): our land, our country

KOOKA (WEMBA WEMBA): grandmother

KUNTHA (KUUKU YA'U) strong

LAGAU KAB: island dance

LAYSH (ABORIGINAL ENGLISH): relation

MAKWARRA KILPARRA (PAAKANTJI/BAAKANTJI): two moieties

MALKARRI (KUUKU YA'U): ceremonial dance

MANA LAKA: old men getting sick

MEPLA: people

MINNA PAWA (TORRES STRAIT CREOLE): appropriate and respectful ways

MURRA KAZIL: everybody

NGAACHI (KUUKU YA'U): homelands, traditional country

NGAATCHI (PAAKANTJI/BAAKANTJI): spirit

NGAI (PAAKANTJI/BAAKANTJI): hello

NINGINAA (YAYGIRR): be quiet

NOONGU (PAAKANTJI/BAAKANTJI): women

NURNA UNTHARLAAPUMA, NGURRALA (NTARIA): we go walking in the late afternoon

NYAKAMU (KUUKU YA'U): phosphorescence

NYANKA (WEMBA WEMBA): grandfather

NYMBALIN: contribute

OOBARR: wongai tree

PITCHENAMMO GWERR (ALYAWAAR): who's that?

PIWU: wallaby (totem)

PULU: grassbird (totem)

PUUYA (KUUKU YA'U): heart

RELHA MAPA (ARRARNTA): our people

RELHA MAPA MARRA NITJIKA (ARRARNTA): our people live well

SAGER: annual wind

TAG MAUKIE MAUKIE (MERIAM MIR): Hands shall not touch another man's land

TAGAI: the sea hero of all Torres Strait Islanders. The star constellation of Tagai gives signs for voyaging, for turtle-mating time, a time for garden preparation.

TETER MAUKIE MAUKIE (MERIAM): feet shall not touch another man's land

THARTU (BARKINDJI/PARKINDJI): head

THOMPWA (ALYAWAAR): old man

TIDDA (ABORIGINAL ENGLISH): sister, woman

TUKULU (KUUKU YA'U): turtle

UPAN: jellyfish (totem)

UTHA LANGU: Indigenous clan name

WAAKU (PAAKANTJI/BAAKANTJI): crow

WAANJI (YAYGIRR): dingo totem

WARRMA (ABORIGINAL ENGLISH): corroborree

WATTAMOOLI: welcome

WHICHAWAY (ABORIGINAL ENGLISH): how are you?

WIIMPATJAS (PAAKANTJI/BAAKANTJI): blackfellas

WIIMPITCHA BAAKANTJI MURLPA KIIRANHA (BARKANJI/PARKANDJI): heartbeat

WIIMPITCHA MURNDY (BARKANJI/PARKANDJI): blackfella country

WINNIANNO (ALYAWAAR): what's that?

WISWEI: which way?

WONGA/WOMBA (ABORIGINAL ENGLISH): crazy

WU'U (KUUKU YA'U): sick

WURTA PMARA MARRA NURNAKA (NTARIA): our country is good

YAAMA (KAMILEROI): welcome

YAANDI (ABORIGINAL ENGLISH): marijuana

YABAA (GAMILARAAY): carpet snake

YABBAS (DJABUGAY): brothers

YAMMA DUMARUNG (WIRADJURI): welcome

YATHU (KUUKU YA'U): children

YAWAI (KUUKU YA'U): that's right

YAWAN: manta ray (totem)

YINDYAMARRA (WIRADJURI): respect

YIRRITJA: All Yolngu people in north-eastern Arnhem Land belong to one of two basic divisions, or moieties, called Dhuwa and Yirritja

YULLIGI YUGUL (GAMILARAAY): traditional song and dance

YUMI (TORRES STRAIT ISLANDER CREOLE): a collective of people, united by a common purpose

YUUTENDALY (GAMILARAAY): sand goanna

ZOGO LE (MERIAM): warrior

BIOGRAPHIES

ELLEN VAN NEERVEN

Ellen van Neerven (born Meanjin, 1990) is an award-winning writer and editor of Mununjali Yugambeh (south-east Queensland) and Dutch heritage. Ellen's fictional debut *Heat and Light*, was the recipient of the David Unaipon Award, the Dobbie Literary Award and the NSW Premier's Literary Awards Indigenous Writers Prize. Ellen is the author of two volumes of poetry, *Comfort Food* and *Throat.*

LAKKARI PITT

Lakkari Pitt is a proud Gamilaroi Yuwalaraay woman from Walgett. Her art explores the movement, essence and stories of country. Lakkari was commissioned as the artist to design and showcase her art for the 2019 Dreamtime Awards, a national awards ceremony that celebrates and recognises Indigenous excellence.

THE COLLI CREW

From the black soil plains of north-west New South Wales, the heart of the Kamileroi Nation, comes a group of 'diminutive, yet razor sharp' rappers from the community of Collarenebri.

Situated on the Barwon River and known as 'The Home of the Cod', Collarenebri is a small community situated about a hundred kilometres from Moree, New South Wales. Desert Pea Media (DPM) began working with Collarenebri Central School in 2011, and over a four-year period created a series of songs and music videos, and two short documentaries.

The Colli Crew performed at events and festivals all over Australia, including the 2011 ARIA Awards (Sydney Opera House), 2013 NRL All-Stars Game (Gold Coast) and the Yabun Festival (Sydney). Their music is still studied around Australia as a part of the New South Wales school curriculum for Indigenous studies. Ten years later, frontman Micheal Graham now creates music as 'Boomalli' and is about to drop his debut album in 2020 with DPM Records.

THE B-TOWN WARRIORS

The B-Town Warriors emerged from a series of DPM storytelling projects with the community of Bourke in New South Wales. Situated on the Darling River, this country represents the borders of the Nyaampa, Barkindji, Wonkamurra, Murrawarri and Kamileroi people.

Thanks to partnerships with Bourke High School and the Vincent Fairfax Family Foundation, the B-Town Warriors and DPM crew have created five songs and music videos over three years. One of the most successful DPM projects ever, the song 'People of the Red Sunset' was played on radio all over Australia, was added to spot rotation on Triple J and received over 500,000 views online.

The B-Town Warriors' track 'Thundercloud' won the National Indigenous Music Award for 'Community Music Clip of the Year' in 2018 in Darwin, Northern Territory.

THE 380 CREW

The Yaegl people are a small, proud and resilient community situated in the Clarence Valley – where the freshwater meets the sea. The mob here have a deep connection with the Clarence River, or 'Biirinba' in the Yaegl language.

DPM worked with the community on three projects in 2018/19 in partnership with Maclean High School and local Yaegl Elders. The 380 Crew is named after a bus route that runs between Yamba and Maclean, and is a key connection between Pippi Beach and Hillcrest – the two major Indigenous communities in the area.

THE LÚRRA COLLECTIVE

Representing fourteen language groups of central-western Arnhem Land, Maningrida is one of the most multilingual places on earth. Over the years it has become a central community for mob from a number of homelands, along both the coastline and the fringing stone country.

Desert Pea Media first engaged with Maningrida in 2014, and worked with the local community on music and film projects on three occasions, in partnership with the Smugglers of Light Foundation, Vincent Fairfax Family Foundation, The Wiwa Project and The Djelk Indigenous Ranger Program, Malabam Health and Maningrida Education Centre.

DESERT PEA MEDIA

Desert Pea Media (DPM) is a small charitable organisation. We have spent the past eighteen years building connections and creating stories with young people, Elders and communities in regional and remote Original Nations communities all over Australia. We would like to respectfully acknowledge the ancestors of all the diverse country upon which DPM learns, shares and creates.

Founded in 2002, the inspiration for Desert Pea Media's process came from an organisation based in Bangkok, in Thailand – 'The Makhampom Foundation' – that works with community and cultural development practice in remote communities around South-East Asia.

Desert Pea Media projects involve a dialogue-based storytelling process that encourages participants to analyse 'the real', 'the ideal' and 'the bridge'. In simple terms, this means critically thinking about how to create positive change for yourself, for each other and for our communities.

In 2003, Matthew Priestley, an acclaimed Kamileroi artist, dancer, filmmaker and director from Moree, New South Wales, joined the DPM family. For the next ten years, co-founders Matthew Priestley and Toby Finlayson worked side-by-side in remote and regional communities around Australia.

ACKNOWLEDGEMENTS

A non-Indigenous organisation, Desert Pea Media (DPM) is very proud of its long history of forming authentic connections and relationships in community. We would like to acknowledge each and every Original Nations community and individual upon whose country we have had the honour to learn, share and create over the past two decades.

We would also like to acknowledge and express our gratitude to all of the partners, funding bodies, host organisations and pro-bono supporters that have enabled the projects themselves, and also the development of this publication. It is an honour to share the poetry and stories of DPM from the past eighteen years in this way, and we are very grateful to Hardie Grant for the opportunity.

We would like to thank the DPM Board of Directors, who volunteer their time and energy to support our work in communities. Your support has enabled us to grow and flourish, and we are eternally grateful for your continuing contributions. A special thanks also to Kylee Ingram, whose contributions to DPM have enabled this publication and inspire us to grow and innovate in an authentic way.

Finally, we would like to congratulate and thank each and every young person and community that has contributed to this body of work. Your stories, and your voice and your ideas are incredibly important to us all, and we thank you for your trust, your energy and your deadliness. All the writing credits are included in the back section.

DESERT
PEA
MEDIA

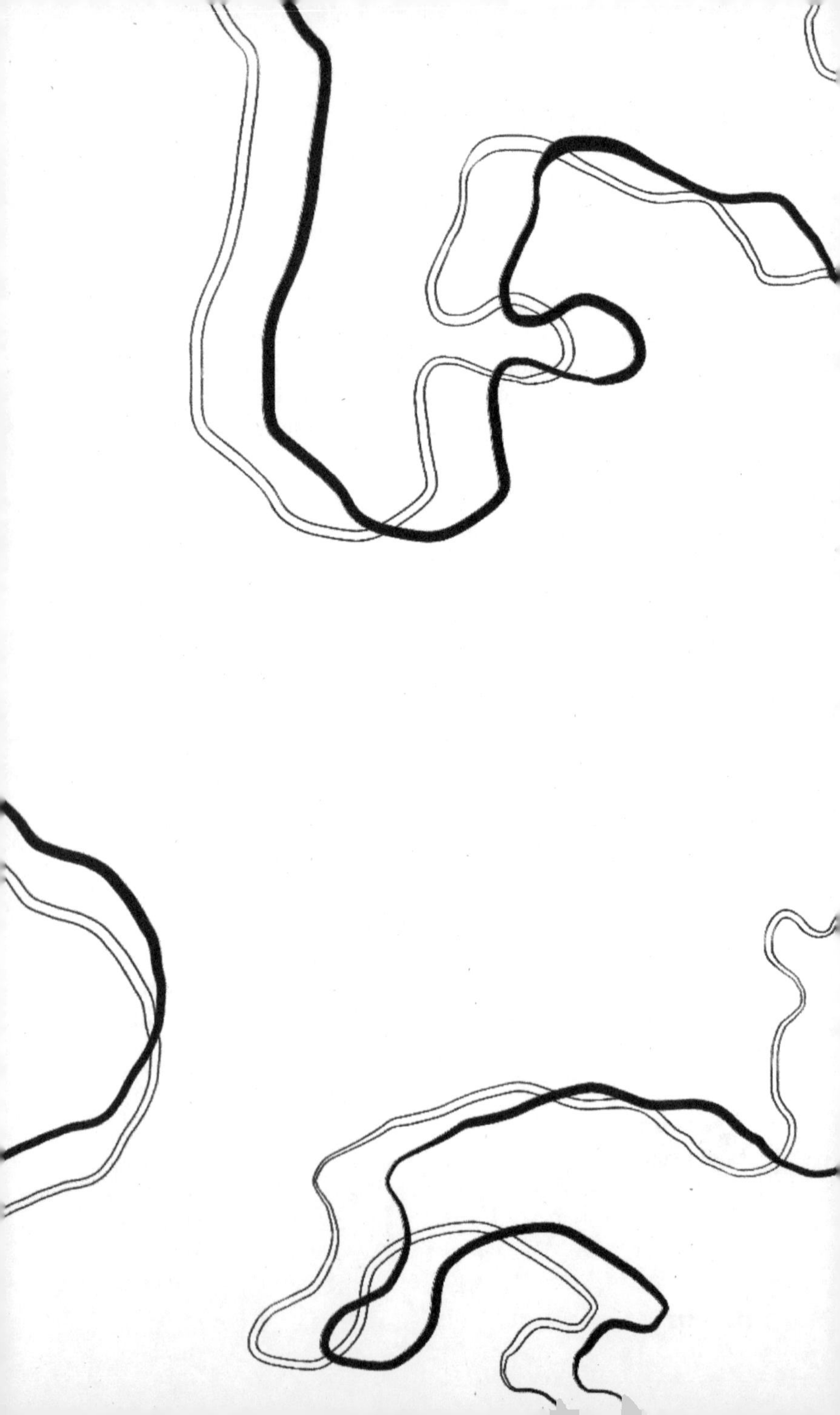

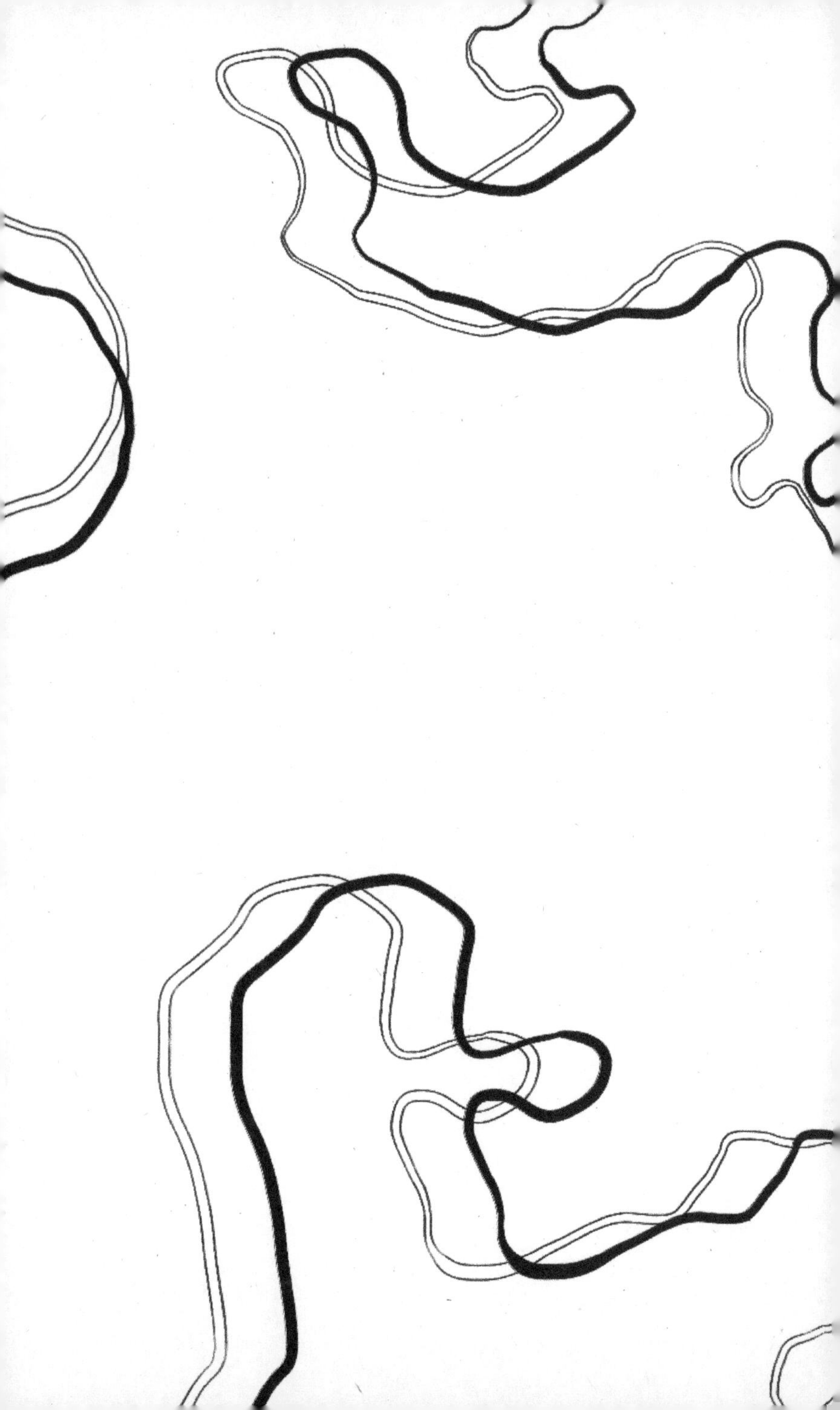